Catalog of
Published Concert Music
by
American Composers

by

Angelo Eagon

Supplement to the Second Edition

The Scarecrow Press, Inc.
Metuchen, N.J.   1971

FOREWORD

The concert music by American composers listed in this Supplement and Addendum to the 2nd Edition of the Catalog of Published Concert Music by American Composers, published by the Scarecrow Press in July 1969, brings the entries up-to-date as of February 1, 1971.

This supplement and the 2nd Edition of the catalog are designed as current references for the extensive repertory of concert music by American composers, including works in various categories which are generally available in some printed form for purchase. Suitable for concert performances, these compositions have been selected for the professional and non-professional musician, for music groups and organizations, schools of music, colleges and universities, libraries and research institutions.

The format and organization follow that of the 2nd Edition.

As stated in the "Foreword" of the 2nd Edition of the catalog, I had planned to include in the First Supplement listings of electronic music or of that music of which a performance relies on mechanical devices, but in my research I found that very few works in that medium are available in any published form for purchase. Many of the works for electronic music are available from various sources, however, on a rental basis. I suggest that those interested in works in this medium contact certain organizations such as The American Music Center, 2109 Broadway, New York, N.Y. 10023; American Composers Alliance, 2121 Broadway, New York, N.Y. 10023; American Society of Composers, Authors and Publishers (ASCAP), 575 Madison Avenue, New York, N.Y. 10022; Broadcast Music, Inc. (BMI), 589 5th Avenue, New York, N.Y. 10017. Other sources would include the music departments of Columbia and Princeton universities and other universities and music schools which maintain libraries of electronic music scores which are probably available on request on a rental basis or in blueprint copies. I have listed those works in which electronic music is used in connection with other instrumental combinations or with voice or with chorus.

Again, I want to express my appreciation for the magnificent assistance I have received from the many music publishers. Such a compilation as this would not have been possible without their cooperation.

Angelo Eagon
Head, Division of Fine Arts
Temple Buell College, Denver, Colorado
February 1, 1971

iii

TABLE OF CONTENTS

---

* With piano unless otherwise indicated
** All durations or timings are approximate

KEY TO ABBREVIATIONS

A	alto voice	E-hn	English horn
acc	accompaniment	fl	flute
acdn	accordion	full	full symphony orchestra
a-cl	alto clarinet	glock	glockenspiel
a-fl	alto flute	gtr	guitar
a-rec or rec(A)	alto recorder	high	high voice
		hn	French horn
a-sax	alto saxophone	har	harmonica
anon	anonymous	hp	harp
B	bass voice	hpcd	harpsichord
b-rec or rec(B)	bass recorder	low	low voice
		man	mandolin
		mar	marimba
Bar	baritone voice	med	medium voice
bar	baritone horn	min	minutes (approximate duration)
bar-sax	baritone saxophone		
B-Bar	bass baritone voice	mov	movement
b-cl	bass clarinet	m-S	mezzo soprano voice
b-dr	bass drum	ms	manuscript
bsn	bassoon	Mu	mute
b-trb	bass trombone	Narr	narrator
clav	clavichord	ob	oboe
c-b	contra bass or double bass	obb	obbligato
c-bsn	contra bassoon	opt	optional
cel	celesta	orch	full orchestra
cent	century	org	organ
ch	chorus	perc	percussion
cham	chamber orchestra	picc	piccolo
cl	clarinet	pno	piano
cmb	cymbals	pt	parts
Col	coloratura voice	(R)	parts on rental
cor	cornet	rec	recorder
dr	drum or drums	rev	revised or revision

S	soprano voice
SATB	mixed chorus (Soprano, Alto, Tenor, Bass)
sax	saxophone
sc	scenes
sn-dr	snare drum
Sp	speaker
s-rec or rec(S)	soprano recorder
SSA	women's chorus (Sopranos I & II, Alto)
str	strings
str qrt	string quartet
susp	suspended
sym	symphony
tam	tambourine
T	tenor voice
t-dr	tenor drum
tba	tuba
timp	timpani
trad	traditional
trans	translator or translation
trb	trombone
tri	triangle
trp	trumpet
t-rec or rec(T)	tenor recorder
t-sax	tenor saxophone
t-trb	tenor trombone
TTBB	men's chorus (Tenors I & II, Basses I & II)
unacc	unaccompanied
vib	vibraphone
vla	viola
vlc	violoncello
vln	violin
xy	xylophone

1. VOICE

SOLO VOCAL MUSIC (Piano Accompaniment Unless Otherwise Indicated)

Composer, Title and Publisher	Range	Author of Text
ADLER, Samuel In thine own image OX	med	Fania Kruger

ARGENTO, Dominick
Six Elizabethan songs B&H
  1. Spring
  2. Sleep
  3. Winter
  4. Dirge
  5. Diaphenia
  6. Hymn
	high	
		Thomas Nashe
		Samuel Daniel
		Shakespeare
		Shakespeare
		Dominick Argento
		Ben Jonson

BAKSA, Robert When the lad for longing sighs B&H	med	A. E. Housman
BECK, John Ness Song of devotion (in: Contemporary Art Songs) GS	med	Biblical
BEESON, Jack Abbie's bird song (from Lizzie Borden) B&H Margaret's garden aria (from Lizzie Borden) B&H	high med	Kenward Elmslie Kenward Elmslie

BINKERD, Gordon
And I am old to know B&H
A bygone occasion B&H
The fair morning B&H
Her definition B&H
If thou wilt ease thine heart B&H
A nursery ode B&H
Peace B&H
Shut out that moon B&H
  1. She, to him
  2. Shut out that moon
  3. A bygone occasion
  4. The riddle
Somewhere I have never travelled
B&H
Three songs for mezzo soprano
and string quartet B&H
  1. Never the nightingale
  2. How lillies came white
  3. Upon parting
	high
	low
	high
	low
	low
	low
	low, high
	high
	
	high
	
	m-S
		Pauline Hanson
		Thomas Hardy
		Jones Very
		Thomas Hardy
		Thomas Beddoes
		Ambrose Phillips
		Henry Vaughan
		Thomas Hardy
		
		e. e. cummings
		
		Adelaide Crapsey
		Robert Herrick
		Robert Herrick

Composer, Title and Publisher	Range	Author of Text
What sweeter musick B&H	low, high	Robert Herrick
The wishing-caps B&H	low	Rudyard Kipling
BLISS, J. A.		
Songs of Omar AMP		Omar Khayyam
Awake	med	
A moment's halt	high	
With me	high	
BOWLES, Paul		
Heavenly grass (in: Contemporary	low	Tennessee Williams
Art Songs) GS		
BURGE, David		
A song of sixpence AB	S	David Burge
CALABRO, Louis		
Macabre reflections (a cycle) EV	m-S	Howard Nemerov
1. The ground swayed		
2. The officer		
3. Each a rose		
4. More than dust		
5. It is forbidden		
6. The sunlight pierced		
CARR, Arthur		
Oriental miniatures WIM	high	Arthur Carr
The evening river. Longing.		
Blue and silver. Moonlight.		
Autumn wind.		
CHADWICK, George (H. Wiley		
Hitchcock, Ed.)		
Songs of George Chadwick (a collec-	varies	
tion of more than 100 songs) DCP		
CHENOWETH, Wilbur		
Vocalise (in: Contemporary Art	med	vocalise
Songs) GS		
CUMBERWORTH, Starling A.		
Three Chinese love lyrics (in:		
Contemporary Art Song Album) GAL	high	Ting Tun-Ling (772-
1. The shadow of a leaf		845); Eng. version by
2. When the sun rose		Gertrude L. Joerissen
3. Tiptoeing to her lover		
CUMMING, Richard		
As dew in April (with ob or vln	high	anon (14th cent)
or cl and pno) B&H		
We happy few (a cycle) B&H	med	
The feast of Crispian		Shakespeare
To whom can I speak today		anon (Egyptian, c. 3000
		BC)
Fife tune		John Manifold
Here dead lie we		A. E. Housman

Composer, Title and Publisher	Range	Author of Text
A ballad of the good Lord Nelson		Lawrence Durrell
Going to the warres		Richard Lovelace
A sight in camp		Walt Whitman
The end of the world		Archibald MacLeish
Grave hour		Rainer Maria Rilke; trans: M. D. Herter Norton
The song of Moses		Biblical
deGASTYNE, Serge		
Sweet spring EV	med	e. e. cummings
DEL TREDICI, David		
I hear an army (with str qrt) B&H	S	No. XXXVI in Chamber Music by James Joyce
Syzygy (with woodwind octet, French horn, 2 trumpets, tabular bells, and string sextet) B&H	S	from "Ecce Puer" and "Nightpiece" by James Joyce
DELLO JOIO, Norman		
Bright star (Light of the world) EBM (See also "Women's Chorus" and "Men's Chorus")	med, high	Norman Dello Joio
Note left on a doorstep EBM	med	Lily Peter
A Christmas carol EBM	med, high	G. K. Chesterton
The holy infant's lullaby EBM	med, high	Norman Dello Joio
DIAMOND, David		
I shall imagine life SMPC	med	e. e. cummings
My papa's waltz SMPC	med	Theodore Roethke
Prayer SMPC	med	Theodore Roethke
DOUGHERTY, Celius		
Heaven-haven CF	med	Gerard Manley Hopkins
Music CF	med	James Russell Lowell
Portrait of a lady CF	low, high	James Russell Lowell
Sound the flute! (in: Contemporary Art Songs) GS	med	William Blake
DUKE, John		
Be still as you are beautiful CF	low, high	Patrick MacDonagh
Magnificat (with org) CF (See alos "Mixed Chorus")	med	liturgical
O world CF	med	Mark van Doren
One red rose CF	med	Mark van Doren
Spring thunder CF	low, high	Mark van Doren
Velvet shoes CF	high	Elinor Wylie
Viennese waltz CF	med, high	Elinor Wylie
When I set out for Lyonnesse CF	low, high	Thomas Hardy
Yellow Hair CF	med	William Butler Yeats
EDMUNDS, John		
The blackbird and the crow CF	low, high	Appalachian folk song
English folk songs CF The bailiff's daughter of Islington Begone dull care. Dabbling in the dew. Early one morning.	low, med, high	trad

Composer, Title and Publisher	Range	Author of Text

Just as the tide was flowing.
The lark in the morning. Love
will find out the way. Praise we
the Lord. Scarborough fair.

Irish folk songs. CF	low, med,	trad
Barney Ross. I know my love.	high	
Lilliburlero.		
Like to the damask rose CF	med	from a Ms. in Christ-church College, Oxford
Music thou soul of Heaven CF	med	from a Ms. in Christ-church College, Oxford
Wexford carol CF	med	trad

FRY,   William Henry (H. Wiley
Hitchcock, Ed.)
Selections from Fry's opera
    Leonora   (1845)   DCP

GABURO, Kenneth
Two (with flute and contrabass acc)   m-S   Virginia Hommel
    TP

GRAHAM, Robert
After a rain at Mokanshan   AMP   med   Witter Bynner

GRANT, Parks
Looking across   AMP   med   Thomas Hardy

GRUENBERG, Louis
Four songs, Op. 24   TP   med
    I went down into the street   Vachel Lindsay
    Larkspur   James Oppenheim
    The plaint of the camel   Charles Edward Carryl
    Stopping by the woods on a   Robert Frost
      snowy evening
    (NOTE: The texts are also
    given in German translation
    by R. St. Hoffmann)

HARTLEY, Walter S.
A Psalm cycle (with fl and pno)   med-high   Biblical
    1. Psalm 63: 1-5
    2. Psalm 12: 1-4
    3. Psalm 43: 1-3
    4. Psalm 40: 1-4
    5. Psalm 145: 1-3; 8-10; 21

HEILNER, Irwin
The traveler   AMP   med   Henry Wadsworth
                                     Longfellow

HITCHCOCK, H. Wiley (Ed.)
The American Musical Miscellany
(Northampton, 1798 - a collection

Composer, Title and Publisher	Range	Author of Text

of 111 songs which were in vogue
   at that time)   DCP   varies
Civil War songs   DCP   varies
Household songs of Stephen Foster   varies
   DCP

HOVHANESS, Alan
   O world   CFP   T or Bar   Percy B. Shelley
                               or B
   Two Shakespeare sonnets, Op. 31   med   Shakespeare
   CFP
    1. When in disgrace with fortune
        and men's eyes.
    2. When to the sessions of sweet
        silent thought.

HUSTON, Scott
   Ante mortem and post mortem GEN   Bar   Robinson Jeffers

IVES, Charles
   Eleven songs and two harmonizations
   (Edited by John Kirkpatrick) AMP

Far from my heavenly home	low	Rev. H. F. Lyte
God bless and keep thee	low	anon
No more	med	William Winter
The one way	med	C. E. Ives
Peaks	med	Henry Bellamann
Pictures	med	Monica Peveril Turnbull
Rock of ages	low	Augustus Montague Toplady
A Scotch lullaby	med	Charles Edmund Merrill, Jr.
A sea dirge	mcd	Shakespeare
There is a certain garden	low	anon
Yellow leaves	low	Henry Bellamann

(The two harmonizations are as follows:)
   Christmas carol   med   Edith Osborne Ives
   In the mornin'   med   Negro spiritual (before
                                   1850) communicated
                                   to Ives in 1929 by
                                   Mary Evelyn Stiles

   Three songs (Edited by John Kirk-   med
      patrick)   AMP
      The greatest man   Anne Collins
      Two little flowers   C. E. Ives
      Where the eagle   M. P. Turnbull

KOCH, Frederick
   Three songs from "The children's set"
   (in: Contemporary Art Song Album)
      GAL   high   Dorothy Aldis
   Whistles.   The sad shoes.
   Rolling down the hill.

KRAUSZ, Susan
   Berceuse (in: Contemporary Art

Composer, Title and Publisher	Range	Author of Text
Song Album) GAL	high	H. L. Rittener; trans: Susan Krausz
LA MONTAINE, John		
The Lord is my Shepherd HWG	med	Biblical
LEES, Benjamin		
Three songs B&H	m-S	
The moonlit tree		Richard Nickson
Close all doors		Richard Nickson
The angel		William Blake
LESSARD, John		
Ariel's song GEN	med	Shakespeare
Full fathom five GEN	med	Shakespeare
Rose cheek'd Laura GEN	med	Thomas Campion
LYBBERT, Donald		
Lines for the fallen (2-pno tuned a quarter-tone apart) CFP	S	William Blake and the Mass for the dead
MacDOWELL, Edward (H. Wiley Hitchcock, Ed.)		
Songs of Edward MacDowell (including the mature songs - Op. 47, 56, 58, 60) DCP	varies	varies
MAYER, William		
Barbara - what have you done? CF (See also "Women's Chorus")	2 S	Susan Otto
Paradox CF	high	Marjorie Marks
MORGENSTERN, Sam		
My apple tree CF	high	Garcia Lorca; trans: Edwin Honig
RAPHLING, Sam		
Autograph album GEN	med	Sam Raphling
Beat! Beat! drums! GEN	med	Walt Whitman
New songs on four romantic poems GEN	med	
Lover's logic		Percy B. Shelley
Gold		Lord Byron
My heart leaps up		William Wordsworth
Splendor in the grass		William Wordsworth
REIF, Paul		
The circus SEM	med	Kenneth Koch
ROREM, Ned		
Catullus: on the burial of his brother B&H	med	Catullus; trans: Aubrey Beardsley
Conversation B&H	med	Elizabeth Bishop
Five poems of Walt Whitman B&H	m-S	Walt Whitman

Composer, Title and Publisher	Range	Author of Text

1. Sometimes with one I love
2. Look down, fair moon
3. Gliding o'er all
4. Reconciliation
5. Gods

Four poems of Tennyson B&H   med   Alfred Lord Tennyson
    Ask me no more. Far-far-away.
    Now sleeps the crimson petal.
    The sleeping palace.

Hearing   B&H   med   Kenneth Koch
    In love with you. Down at the
      docks.
    Poem. Spring. Invitation. Hearing.

Love B&H   med   Thomas Lodge
Some trees (a cycle)   B&H   S, m-S, Bar   John Ashbery
    Some trees.   The grapevine.
    Our youth.

Sun (eight poems in one mov.)   high
    (orch(R))   B&H
    1. To the sun   King Ikhnaton, c. 1360
                           B. C.; trans: Ned
                           Rorem
    2. Sun of the sleepless   Lord Byron
    3. To dawn   Paul Goodman
    4. Day   William Blake
    5. Catafalque   Robin Morgan
    6. Sonnet XXXIII   Shakespeare
    7. Sundown lights   Walt Whitman
    8. From "What can I tell my bones" Theodore Roethke
Three incantations from a marionette   med   Charles Boultenhouse
    tale   B&H
    (see also "Mixed Chorus")
Three poems of Demetrios Cape-   med   Demetrios Capetanakis
    tanakis   B&H
    Able. Guilt. The land of fear.
Three poems of Paul Goodman B&H   med   Paul Goodman
    Clouds. For Susan. What sparks
      and wiry cries.
Two poems of Theodore Roethke B&H med   Theodore Roethke
    I strolled across an open field.
    Orchids.

ROY, Klaus George
    Holiday (in: Contemporary Art   high   Adrienne Rich
    Song Album)   GAL

SACCO, P. Peter
    Three Psalms (with brass quintet) WIM   T   Biblical

SARGENT, Paul
    Stopping by the woods on a snowy   med   Robert Frost
    evening (in: Contemporary Art
    Songs)   GS

SCHRAMM, Harold
    Song of Tāyumānavar (with fl) TP   S   Tāyumānavar (16th or
                            17th century)

Composer, Title and Publisher	Range	Author of Text

SCHUMAN, William
  Holiday song (in: Contemporary
  Art Songs)   GS
	med	Genevieve Taggard

SMITH, Hale
  Beyond the rim of day   EBM
    1. March moon
    2. Troubled woman
    3. To a little lover-lass, dead
	high	Langston Hughes

SMITH, Julia
  Three love songs   TP
  The door that I would open.
  The love I hold.   I will sing
  the song.
	low, med, high	Karl Flaster

WHITE, John
  A cradle song (in: Contemporary
  Art Song Album)   GAL
	high	William Blake

MIXED CHORUS (SATB a cappella unless otherwise indicated)

Composer, Title and Publisher	Chorus	Solos	Accompaniment	Author of Text
ADLER, Samuel				
The feast of lights GS			pno	E. Guthmann
Judah's song of praise GS			pno	Samuel Adler
A kiss AMP				Austin Dobson
Psalm 40 OX			org	Biblical
Psalm 44 PIC				Biblical
Wisdom cometh with the years PIC			orch(R)	Countee Cullen
ARGENTO, Dominick				
A nation of cowslips B&H				Doggerel verses
1. The Devon maid				from John
2. On visiting Oxford				Keats' letters
3. Sharing Eve's apple				written during
4. There was a naughty boy				his travels through Eng-
5. A party of lovers at tea				land
6. Two or three posies				
7. In praise of Apollo				
AVSHALOMOV, Jacob				
Wonders MCA				William Blake
BALLARD, Louis W.				
The gods will hear (a choral cantata) BI	S, A, T, B		pno & perc	Lloyd H. New
BARBER, Samuel				
Lamb of God (transcribed from "Adagio for strings", Op. 11) GS				Biblical
On the death of Cleopatra (from "Two choruses from Antony and Cleopatra") GS (See also "Women's Chorus")			pno	Shakespeare
To be sung on the water GS				Louise Bogan
Twelfth night GS				Laurie Lee
BARTOW, Nevett				
The tower of Babel (cantata) SHAW			pno & perc	Free and contemporary
I. Introduction				adaptations
II. The building of the tower				from the Bible
III. God's judgement: the confusion of tongues				
IV. Finale				
BAUMGARTNER, H. Leroy				
The city (choral suite)ECS SSATBB				
1. The city's crown				William Dudley Foulke

Composer, Title and Publisher	Chorus	Solos	Accompaniment	Author of Text
2. The metropolis				Thomas Caldecot Chubb
3. In the city				Israel Zangwill
4. Calm soul of things				Matthew Arnold
5. The city				Frank Mason North
BEESON, Jack				
Three settings from The Bay Psalm Book OX (Psalms 23, 47, 131)				Biblical
Tides of Miranda (madrigal)				Sarah Moore
OX	SSATB			
BEGLARIAN, Grant				
....And all the hills echoed (a cantata) EBM		B-Bar, Narr	org and timp	Biblical
BELCHER, Supply (H. Wiley Hitchcock, Ed.)				
The harmony of Maine (Boston, 1794) DCP				
BENNETT, David				
The spirit of music CF			pno	David Bennett
BENSON, Warren				
An Englishman with an atlas or America the unpronounceable MCA	SAB			Morris Bishop
Love is MCA	SSAATTBB			May Swenson
Rondino for 8 hand clappers EBM		for any group of 8 musicians from chorus, band or orch.		
BERKOWITZ, Leonard				
Four songs on poems of Emily Dickinson (published separately) AMP				Emily Dickinson
Hope. I'm nobody. I never saw a moor. The wind.				
BERKOWITZ, Sol				
Without words (suite) CHAP				vocalise
Repetitions. Dance song. Sweet lament. Cross talk				
BERLINSKI, Herman				
It hath been told thee, O man TP			org	Biblical

Composer, Title and Publisher	Chorus	Solos	Accompaniment	Author of Text

BERRY, Wallace
  No man is an island SMPC   pno   John Donne

BILLINGS, William
  (H. Wiley Hitchcock, Ed.)
  The New England Psalm
    Singer (Boston, 1770) DCP

BINKERD, Gordon

	Chorus	Solos	Accompaniment	Author of Text
Autumn flowers B&H	SSATB			Jones Very
Ave Maria B&H				liturgical
A birthday B&H				Christina Rossetti
A Christmas carol B&H	SSAATBB			Robert Herrick
Compleynt, compleynt B&H				Ezra Pound
Confitebor tibi B&H				Liber Usualis
Epitaphs B&H				Ezra Pound
Eternitie B&H	SSATB			Robert Herrick
Garden B&H				Carlton Lowenberg
Huswifery B&H				Edward Taylor
In a whispering gallery B&H				Thomas Hardy
Institutional canons B&H				
Jesus weeping B&H	SSAATBB			Henry Vaughan
The last invocation B&H				Walt Whitman
Memorial B&H			pno	Richard Crashaw
Nocturne (with solo cello) B&H	SSAATBB			William Carlos Williams
Omnes gentes B&H				Liber Usualis
Salutis humanae sator B&H				Liber Usualis
To Electra B&H				Robert Herrick
1. I dare not ask a kisse	SSATB			
2. Love looks for love	SSSAA			
3. More white than whitest lillies far	SSSAATBB			
4. 'Tis ev'ning, my sweet	STB			
5. Upon Electra's teares				
We in this whirl are caught B&H				Rainer Maria Rilke;trans: Ludwig Lewisohn
The work B&H				Neil Weiss

BLAKLEY, D. Duane

	Chorus	Solos	Accompaniment	Author of Text
Jesus Christ, the Crucified (a contemporary cantata) SHAW		S,A,T, B, Narr	org; or brass qrt and perc	Biblical and trad

Composer, Title and Publisher	Chorus	Solos	Accompaniment	Author of Text
BLITZSTEIN, Marc				
Invitation to bitterness B&H	ATB			Marc Blitzstein
This is the garden (a cantata of New York) CHAP			orch(R)	Marc Blitzstein
1. The Lex express				
2. I'm ten and you'll see				
3. Harlan Brown, killed in the street				
4. Hymie is a poop				
5. In twos				
6. San Gennaro				
BOERINGER, James				
On the morning of Christ's nativity (Christmas cantata) Introduction (org). It was the winter wilde (ch). No war, or battails sound (S or T solo). But peaceful was the night (ch). The shepherds on the lawn (ch). Such musick (S or T solo). Ring out ye crystall spheres (ch). For if such holy song (S or T solo). Yea truth, and justice then (ch). With such a horrid clang (ch). And then at last our bliss (S or T solo). But see the Virgin blest (ch).	JF	S or T	org	John Milton
BOYD, Jack				
All has been heard L-G				Biblical
Three contemplations of Ann Bradstreet WLP				Ann Bradstreet
BRIGHT, Houston				
Premonition SHAW				Houston Bright
Seaweed SHAW				Henry Wadsworth Longfellow
Softly flow the midnight hours SHAW				Houston Bright
Soliloquy SHAW	SSAATTBB			Alfred Lord Tennyson
Vision of Isaiah SHAW	SSAATTBB		org or orch(R)	Biblical
1. I saw the Lord				
2. And the posts of the door moved				
3. Then said I, woe is me				

Composer, Title and Publisher	Chorus	Solos	Accompaniment	Author of Text
When the lamp is shattered SHAW				Percy B. Shelley
BROWN, Rayner Aus tiefer Not (Psalm 130) WIM	A		org	Biblical
BRUBECK, Dave Choruses from The Light in the Wilderness (published separately) SHAW Forty days			org with opt perc and c-b	Dave and Iola Brubeck
Let not your heart be troubled		Bar		
Praise ye the Lord				
The sermon on the mount				
(For complete contents of The Light in the Wilderness, see Second Edition of this Catalog, p. 60-61)				
BUCCI, Mark The wondrous kingdom (flora and fauna) MCA				
1. Prelude				William Blake
2. The sunflower				William Blake
3. The lamb				William Blake
4. The rose tree				William Blake
5. The tiger				William Blake
6. The squirrel				Ralph Waldo Emerson
7. The mustard seed				Biblical
8. The birds				William Blake
9. Postlude				George Herbert
CARDEN, Allen (H. Wiley Hitchcock, Ed.) The Missouri harmony (a collection of revival music of folk hymns: Cincinnati, 1820) DCP				
CARTER, John The cloths of Heaven FM				William Butler Yeats
CHAPPELL, Herbert The Daniel jazz EBM	unison		pno	Vachel Lindsay
CLARKE, Henry Leland L'allergo and Il penseroso TP				John Milton
COHN, John Statues in the park CF				Felicia Lampert

Composer, Title and Publisher	Chorus	Solos	Accompaniment	Author of Text
Point of view. Equable explanation. Dress parade. Bronx River puzzle. Monumental paradox. Who he? The gamut. Technical advice to persons planning to erect memorial statues to themselves.				
COWELL, Henry Ultimo actio AMP	SSATB			José De Diego; trans: Joseph Machlis
CROOKS, Mack December carol L-G				Joseph Ehreth
DALLIN, Leon Songs of praise MCA		A, T	orch(R) or band(R)	Biblical
1. O praise the Lord (Psalm 117)		A		
2. Come unto Me (Men's ch)		T		
3. Love the Lord (Psalm 116)				
4. Praise God (Psalms 147, 150)				
DAVIS, Katherine K. The tyger GAL			pno	William Blake
DAVISON, John Lo, this land EBM			pno or org or band(R), or orch(R)	Walt Whitman
DELLO JOIO, Norman Evocations EBM			pno or orch(R)	
1. Visitants at night				Robert Hillyer
2. Promise of spring				Richard Hovey
Mass EBM			org and brass(R)	liturgical
Years of the modern EBM			brass and perc	Walt Whitman
DEL TREDICI, David Pop-Pourri B&H		amplified S solo (and counter-tenor or m-S ad lib)	amplified solo-rock group of 2 sax and 2 electric gtr and orch(R)	from Alice in Wonderland by Lewis Carroll and the Litany of the Blessed Virgin Mary

Composer, Title and Publisher	Chorus	Solos	Accompaniment	Author of Text

DENNISON, Sam
  The faucon hath taken
    my mate away AMP
				anon (Middle
				  Eng.)

DIAMOND, David
  To music (choral sym-
    phony) SMPC
  I. Invocation to music
  II. Symphonic affirma-
      tion
  III. Dedication
	tacit	T, B-
		Bar
			orch(R)	
				John Masefield
				
				Henry Wads-
				  worth
				  Longfellow

Two anthems   SMPC
    To Thee, O Lord.
    Why the fuss?
				Biblical

DIEMER, Emma Lou
  At a solemn music   B&H
  Now the spring has come
    again   B&H
			
			pno
				John Milton
				from Piae Can-
				  tiones (1582);
				  trans: Steuart
				  Wilson

Shepherd to his love EBM			fl and pno	Christopher Marlowe

Verses from the Rubaiyat
    B&H
    1. Myself when young
        did eagerly frequent
    2. With them the seed
        of wisdom did I sow
    3. Here with a loaf of
        bread beneath the
        bough
    4. There was the door
        to which I found
        no key
    5. Come, fill the cup,
        and in the fire of
        spring
				Omar Khayyam;
				  trans: Edward
				  Fitzgerald

DIERCKS, John
  Why do the nations
    rage? (Psalm 2) ABP
			pno or
			org
				Biblical

DOHERTY, Anthony A song of joy WLP				Walt Whitman
DONAHUE, Bertha Terry Make we joy AMP				15th cent. carol
DOUGHERTY, Celius A minor bird GS			pno	Celius Dougherty

Composer, Title and Publisher	Chorus	Solos	Accompaniment	Author of Text
DRAESEL, Jr. and H. Bruce Lederhouse				
Celebration (mass with a rock beat) EBM	unison		gtr, org (or pno), dr	liturgical
Praise and Jubilee (a contemporary mass) EBM	unison		org	liturgical
Rejoice (mass in contemporary country-folk style) EBM	unison		gtr, org (or pno)	liturgical
DROSTE, Doreen When you are old AMP			pno	William Butler Yeats
DUKE, John Magnificat CF (See also "Solo Vocal")	unison		org	liturgical
DUNFORD, Benjamin The unspeakable gift (a Christmas cantata) JF	SAB	Bar	org (instr. acc. opt: 3 trp, 3 trb, tba, timp, perc)	Biblical
The word and the prophecy. The prophecy fulfilled. The message of the angel. The star and the adoration. The unspeakable gift. Psalm 103 JF		Bar	org (instr. acc. opt: 2 hn, 3 trp, 3 trb, tba, timp, perc)	Biblical
A song of personal praise. An anthem of world-wide praise. A symphony of universal praise. A song of personal praise.				
DVORAK, Robert Songs of deliverance (a cantata) COL		Narr	brass, perc, str (R)	Biblical
ESCOVADO, Robin Psalm 131 AMP				Biblical
FAST, Willard S. Autumn EV				Rainer Maria Rilke
FELDMAN, Morton Chorus and instruments (II) CFP			chimes, tba	vocalise

Composer, Title and Publisher	Chorus	Solos	Accompaniment	Author of Text
The swallows of Salangan CFP			7vlc, 4 fl, a-fl, 5 trp, 2 tba, 2 vib, 2 pno (R)	vocalise
FETLER, Paul				
A contemporary Psalm AUG (See also "Percussion")		S, Bar	org and perc(R)	Chester A. Pennington
Wild swans AMP				Edna St. Vincent Millay
FISSINGER, Edwin				
O make a joyful noise (Psalm 66) AMP				Biblical
Star that I see WLP The star that I see. Moon magic. Winter wren. Dandelions. Will you remember?				Leigh Hanes
FLAGELLO, Nicolas				
Te deum for all mankind CF			pno or orch(R)	Latin liturgy and "Laus Deo" by John Greenleaf Whittier
FLOYD, Carlisle				
Two Choruses from Passion of Jonathan Wade B&H Down in Galilee Free as a frog				Anon
FORCUCCI, Samuel L.				
Child of wonder (cantata for the Christmas season) AMP 1. In bleak midwinter 2. Our God 3. Before Whom angels bow 4. Angels and archangels 5. Alleluia and chorale		S, T	pno, 4-hands	Christina Rossetti
FOSS, Lukas				
Adon Olom (The Lord of all) GS			org	Lukas Foss
FOX, Fred				
The look GAL				Sara Teasdale
It pays GAL				Arnold Bennett

Composer, Title and Publisher	Chorus	Solos	Accompaniment	Author of Text
FRACKENPOHL, Arthur				
Cheer up EBM			pno	anon
Hogamus, higamus SAB	SAB		perc	anon
(double fugue for speaking chorus and perc) EBM (See also "Women's Chorus", "Men's Chorus" and "Percussion")				
My song forever shall record (Psalm 89) EBM				Biblical
Oh, breathe not His name EBM			pno	Sir Thomas Moore
FREED, Arnold				
Heaven-haven B&H				Gerard Manley Hopkins
Three shepherd carols B&H				anon
Angels we have heard on high. O come to Bethlehem. Shepherds! shake off your drowsy sleep.				
FULLER, Jeanne Weaver				
Exsultate, justi (Psalm 32) AMP				Biblical
Now (more near ourselves than we) AMP			pno	e.e. cummings
GAMBOLD, John (arr. and edited by Ewald V. Nolte)				
Who with weeping soweth (Psalm 126) B&H	SATB or SSAB		org	Biblical
GLASS, Philip				
The last invocation EV				Walt Whitman
GOEMANNE, Noel				
Entrata (Psalm 99) WLP			org or 3 trp, 2 trb, timp	Biblical
GOODMAN, Joseph				
Adoremus Te, Christe AMP				liturgical
Crucem tuam adoremus AMP				liturgical
GORE, Richard T.				
Psalm diptych (Psalms 50 and 150) JF			org	Biblical
GRUNDMAN, Clare				
Three noels B&H Christmas hymn.	SATB or SAB		pno	trad

Composer, Title and Publisher	Chorus	Solos	Accompaniment	Author of Text
Christmas eve is here. Now we sing of Christmas. (See also "Women's Chorus" and "Men's Chorus")				
HAGEMANN, Philip				
The musical menagerie TP			pno	Ogden Nash
The fly. The kitten. The lion. Glossina morsitans, or, the tsetse. The termite. The eel. The ostrich. The firefly. The duck. The mermaid. The octopus.				
HANSON, Howard				
The mystic trumpeter CF		Narr	orch(R)	Walt Whitman
Streams in the desert CF			pno or orch(R)	Biblical
Two Psalms (Nos. 121 and 150) CF			org or orch(R)	Biblical
HARTLEY, Walter S.				
How excellent Thy name GAL				Biblical
O sing a new song MCA	SSATB			Biblical
HASLAM, Herbert				
Special starlight TP	SATB with treble voices	Narr	orch(R)	Carl Sandburg
HAYWARD, Lou				
Concert vocalise SHAW		S, A, B	pno or hpcd	vocalise
HENSEL, Richard				
Three songs on poems of Edwin Arlington Robinson WLP				Edwin Arlington Robinson
Cliff Klingenhagen. James Wetherell. Reuben Bright.				
HERDER, Ronald				
The Job elegies AMP				Biblical
HOIBY, Lee				
Ascension TP			pno or org	John Donne
Inherit the Kingdom TP		Bar	org	Biblical
Let this mind be in you TP			org	Biblical

Composer, Title and Publisher	Chorus	Solos	Accompaniment	Author of Text
HOPSON, Hal				
Canticle of praise SHAW			org and 3 trp (opt)	Adapted from Psalms and St. Francis of Assisi; trans: William Draper
HOVHANESS, Alan				
Behold, God is my help CFP		BAR	org or pno	Biblical
I will lift up mine eyes (Psalm 121) (cantata) CFP		B ad lib	org	Biblical
Keep not Thou silence (Psalm 83) AMP				Biblical
The Lord is my shepherd (Psalm 23) CFP			org or pno or 6 vln	Biblical
Make a joyful noise (cantata) CFP Prelude. Save me, O God. Give ear to my prayer. Make His praise glorious.		T or Bar	2 trp, 2 trb, org	Biblical
O Lord God of Hosts CFP			org or pno or 2 trp, 2 trb, ad lib	Biblical
HUNKINS, Arthur				
Libera nos B&H				liturgical
HUNKINS, Eusebia				
Americana CF			pno or orch(R) or band(R)	Eusebia Hunkins
HURD, Michael				
Jonah-man jazz EBM	unison		pno	Biblical
HUSTED, Benjamin				
Snow storm WLP			pno	Ralph Waldo Emerson
IVES, Charles				
Circus band PIC			cham(R)	Charles Ives
JARRETT, Jack				
Choral symphony on American poems CF			pno or orch(R) or band(R)	
Concord hymn				Ralph Waldo Emerson
The statue of old Andrew Jackson				Vachel Lindsay
Out of May's shows	unison			Walt Whitman
In praise of Johnny Appleseed				Vachel Lindsay

Composer, Title and Publisher	Chorus	Solos	Accompaniment	Author of Text
The manger L-G	SAB			Lizette Woodworth Reece
Under the greenwood tree BI			pno	Shakespeare
Who is Sylvia? BI			pno	Shakespeare
JOHNS, Donald				
Magnificat WIM		S	org	Biblical
JOHNSON, Gordon				
Seven Japanese tanka EBM				Kenneth Rexroth
1. Mist				
2. In the spring				
3. Pearls				
4. White egret				
5. Recalled				
6. A doe				
7. Fondly				
JOHNSTON, Jack				
Sweet was the song the Virgin sang EV	SAB			William Ballet (17th cent)
JONES, George Sykes				
In a strange land (Psalm 137) SHAW				Biblical
JONES, Robert W.				
Hist whist (with bass and snare drums, triangle, cymbal) SHAW	SATB choric speech		orch(R) opt	e.e. cummings
Magnificat and nunc dimittis HWG			org, 3 trp, 3 trb, timp	liturgical
A Psalm of praise (Psalm 117) L-G			org	Biblical
KALMANOFF, Martin				
Sermon on the mount MCA			pno	Biblical
KEATS, Donald				
anyone lived in a pretty how town B&H	SSATBB			e. e. cummings
KECHLEY, Gerald				
"The dwelling of youth" CF			band(R)	Gerald Kechley after ancient Sanskrit
In the lonely midnight TP				T.C. Williams
Psalm 121 TP				Biblical
Thank we now the Lord of Heaven TP				Henry Hawkes (based on the plain-song "Divinum Mysterium")

Composer, Title and Publisher	Chorus	Solos	Accompaniment	Author of Text
KENNEDY, John Brodbin Rise, my soul, and stretch thy wings B&H	SAB		org	Robert Seagrave
KENT, Richard Chaconne for chorus (Proverbs) WLP				Biblical
In the bleak midwinter AUG			pno	Christina Rossetti
KEYES, Nelson All is safe EV				Kenneth Patchen
Give you a lantern EV				Kenneth Patchen
KING, Alvin Psalm 47 ("O clap your hands, all ye people") AUG		Narr	4 trp, 2 trb, hn, tba	Biblical
KIRCHNER, Leon Words from Wordsworth AMP				William Wordsworth
KIRK, Theron I will give thanks SHAW				Biblical
O clap your hands (Psalm 47) SHAW			org	Biblical
O sons and daughters JF			org, trp, tba, timp	from a French carol; trans: J. M. Neale
Rejoice in the land (Psalm 33) EBM			2 trp, pno or org	Biblical
Sing for joy EBM			org and pno and opt: 2 trp, 2 trb	Biblical
Three chorales in modern style JF Jesus Lord, Precious Savior				John Wallin
O darkest woe				Johann Rist
O Christ, our hope				Latin (17th cent)
Triptych of psalms NAK Great is the Lord. Lord, I call upon Thee. O sing unto the Lord.				Biblical
KLEIN, Lothar Three laments WLP				from anon Chinese poets
Clean is the autumn wind. The white moon is rising. Who sits alone.				

Composer, Title and Publisher	Chorus	Solos	Accompaniment	Author of Text
KLEINSINGER, George I hear America singing (a cantata) EBM		Bar	pno or orch(R)	Walt Whitman

For the brood beyond us.
  Interlink'd, food-yielding
  lands.   And for the past.
  See, steamers steaming.
  Ode to Democracy.				

KNEALE, Peter Lute book lullaby MCA			gtr or pno	William Ballet (17th cent)
KORTE, Karl Aspects of love ECS				
1. Rise up, my love				Song of Solomon
2. Shall I?	SA		pno	Sappho
3. I will make you brooches			pno	Robert Louis Stevenson
4. Marriage	SA, TB or SATB		pno	Ralph Waldo Emerson
5. Wine of the grape		T	pno	Li T'ai Po (T'ang dynasty); trans: Henry H. Hart
6. Bitter is my lot	TTB			Shao Ch'ang Heng(Ch'ing dynasty); trans: H. H. Hart
7. Jenny kiss'd me	TB		pno	Leigh Hunt

8. My silks and fine
     array (all songs
     available only separately)
			pno	William Blake

O, give thanks (Psalm 136) GAL			pno	Biblical
KRAEHENBUEHL, David City scene WLP				David Kraehenbuehl
KREUTZ, Robert Wind from the West WLP				Ella Young
KROEGER, Karl Dies sanctificatus (This sacred day) L-G				Liber Usualis
KUBIK, Gail A Christmas offering B&H Hymn				Sidney Godolphin (17th cent)
Make we joye nowe in this fest		T and solo qrt (SATB)		anon (15th cent)

Composer, Title and Publisher	Chorus	Solos	Accompaniment	Author of Text
A Christmas set MCA			cham(R)	
1. "What tydyngs bryngest thou massanger?"				anon (15th cent)
2. Lullay, lullay, litel child				anon (14th cent)
3. All this night, shrill chauntecleere				William Austin
4. An hymne				Phineas Fletcher
5. Allon, gay, gay, gay bergeres				Guillaume Costeley
LADERMAN, Ezra				
The trials of Galileo (an oratorio) OX		A, 2 T, counter-tenor, 2 Bar, B	orch(R)	Joe Darion
LANE, Richard				
A hymn to the night MIL				Henry Wadsworth Longfellow
LAW, Andrew (H. Wiley Hitchcock, Ed.)				
Select harmony (Farmington, 1779) DCP				
LEICH, Roland				
XXth century SHAW				Robert Hillyer
LEKBERG, Sven				
Four carols for a holy night GS				Sven Lekberg
Sing noel. Earth so lovely. The little boy Jesus. These are the blossoms.				
Lord of the earth and sky (a cantata) GS		S, Bar (or A)	pno	
Lord of the earth and sky				ancient prayer
Carol				William Austin
The lamb				William Blake
A voice sings				Samuel Taylor Coleridge
I see His blood upon the rose				Joseph Plunkett
A Christmas carol				Christina Rossetti
An ancient Irish hymn				anon
LITTLE, William & William Smith (H. Wiley Hitchcock, Ed.)				
The easy instructor (First collection of American music in the unique "shape note" notation) DCP				

Composer, Title and Publisher	Chorus	Solos	Accompaniment	Author of Text
LOCKWOOD, Normand This moment yearning and thoughtful WLP				Walt Whitman
LOJEWSKI, Harry V. Mass: Americana WLP			org & gtr	Bishops' Committee on the Liturgy
Lord, have mercy. I believe in one God. Holy, holy, holy. Lamb of God.				
LO PRESTI, Ronald Alleluia! Christus natus est CF			pno or org or brass ensemble	liturgical
LOWENBERG, Kenneth The liturgy of the Lord's supper HWG Kyrie. Gloria in excelsis. The presentation. Sanctus. Christ our Passover.	unison		org	liturgical
LUBOFF, Norman African mass WMC Kyrie. Gloria. Credo. Sanctus. Benedictus. Agnus Dei. (See also "Percussion")			tuned dr	liturgical
MADER, Clarence The fifth mystery (cantata) WIM			org	Clarence Mader
I. Who could know		Narr, S, A, B		
II. The cross		Narr, T		
III. The tomb		Narr, A		
IV. The third day		Narr		
MAILMAN, Martin Concord hymn MIL			hp or pno or gtr band (R)	Ralph Waldo Emerson
The whalemen's chorale from "Moby Dick" (the chorus in this work for band is optional) MIL (See also "Band")				Herman Melville
MARTIRANO, Salvatore O, O, O, O, that Shakespeherian rag AMP 1. Winter (Love's Labor Lost)			pno or cl, sax, trp, trb, c-b, pno, perc	Shakespeare

Composer, Title and Publisher	Chorus	Solos	Accompaniment	Author of Text
2. Lullaby (A Midsummer Night's Dream) (SSA)				
3. Warning (The Tempest) (TTBB)				
4. Spring (Love's Labor Lost) (See also "Women's Chorus" and "Men's Chorus")				
MAYER, William				
Letters home MCA		m-S, T, Narr	pno or orch(R)	texts consist largely of authentic letters from soldiers fighting in Vietnam
McAFEE, Don				
A choric psalm CF (See also "Percussion")	speaking ch		perc	Biblical
Contemporary Christmas carols CF				Richard Lamb
Carol of the New Year. The Christmas tree. Little town. Minute carol. Peace carol. (All available only separately)				
I'll tell you how the sun rose EV				Emily Dickinson
The sermon on the Mount JF			pno or org	Biblical
Prologue. The Beatitudes. The light of the world. Jesus' attitude toward the law. Love of enemies. On prayer. The Lord's prayer. Ask, seek, knock. Wise and foolish builders. Epilogue.				
Songs of praise from early America (edited by Don McAfee) BI				
Two parables CF				Biblical
The good samaritan. Parable of the sower.				
McKay, David				
i thank you god JF	SAB		org	e.e. cummings
MECHEM, Kirke				
The ballad of Befana (An Epiphany legend) ECS			gtr	Phyllis McGinley

Composer, Title and Publisher	Chorus	Solos	Accompaniment	Author of Text
Christmas carol ECS			gtr	Sara Teasdale
MILLER, Lewis M.				
To the moon EV				Percy B. Shelley
River run EV				Clare Aguirre
MIRANTE, Thomas				
The house on the hill **AMP**			pno	Edwin Arlington Robinson
I am **AMP**			pno	John Clare
MOEVS, Robert				
A brief mass for the new church EBM			cham orch(R)	liturgical
Itaque ut EBM	SSAT			Catullus
MUCZYNSKI, Robert				
Alleluia GS				liturgical
I never saw a moor GS				Emily Dickinson
NELSON, Ron				
God, bring Thy sword **B&H**			org (perc opt)	Samuel H. Miller
OLSON, Robert G.				
Break forth in song SHAW				from "Centennial Hymn" by John Pierpont
O'NEAL, Barry				
A grain of sand (Choral elegy) **AMP**	divisi			Barry O'Neal
OWEN, Harold				
Metropolitan bus (a cantata) **WIM** These are the words. No smoking. Unnecessary conversation. Emergency exit. Watch your step. Conclusion.			pno (4-hands)	Harold Owen
PAPALE, Henry				
A choral miscellany **WLP**				
Day				William Blake
Follow the gleam				Alfred Lord Tennyson
Full fadom five				Shakespeare
Hey robin				Shakespeare
PENINGER, David				
Let all on earth their voices raise JF			org or brass (opt)	Isaac Watts

Composer, Title and Publisher	Chorus	Solos	Accompaniment	Author of Text
PERSICHETTI, Vincent				
The creation (oratorio) EV		S, A, T, B	orch(R)	Vincent Persi-
I. Darkness and light		Bar, S		chetti based
II. Let there be a firmament		A, T		on texts from
III. I will multiply your seed		S (T-Bar)		mythological,
IV. Lights for seasons		Bar (T-S)		scientific,
V. Of sea and air		A (T-S)		poetic and
VI. After His kind		S, A, T, Bar		Biblical
VII. Behold His glory		S, A, T, Bar		sources
The pleiades EV			trp and str	Walt Whitman
			orch(R) or	
			org & trp or	
			pno & trp or	
			pno (3-hands)	
PFAUTSCH, Lloyd				
Triptych L-G				
1. Musicks empire				Andrew Marvell
2. Orpheus and his lute				Shakespeare
3. Consecrate the place and day				Joseph Addison
PILLIN, Boris				
So gehst du nun		S, A, T	org	Biblical
(a cantata) WIM				
Lord Jesus, Thou art going forth				
O soul, affend thou and behold		T		
O soul, I take upon me now		S & A duet		
What can I for such love devine				
PINKHAM, Daniel				
How precious is Thy loving kindness CFP				Biblical
I was glad (Psalm 122) AMP				Biblical
Prelude, adagio and chorale CFP	unison		2 trp, hn, trb, tba	Daniel Pinkham
Psalm set CFP			org or pno or 2 trp, 2 trb	Biblical
Fanfare (Psalm 134)				
Benediction (Psalm 117)				
Jubilation (Psalm 47)				
Sometimes the soul ECS			pno, gtr	Norma Farber
PISTON, Walter				
Bow down Thine ear, O Lord (Psalm 86) AMP			pno	Biblical
O sing unto the Lord a new song (Psalm 96) AMP			pno	Biblical

Composer, Title and Publisher	Chorus	Solos	Accompaniment	Author of Text
POLIFRONE, Jon 3 madrigals AMP				Helen Louise Quig
Two little ladies. I gave to love. Maiden prithee.				
PURVIS, Richard A psalm of ascents (Psalm 121) MCA			org, trp (opt)	Biblical
De profundis (Psalm 130) MCA			org, trp (opt)	Biblical
Jubilate Deo MCA	unison			liturgical
Unto us a child is born MCA			org, trp (opt)	Biblical
PYLE, Francis Johnson Full stature ABP			pno or org	Iva Durham Vennard
I have chosen Thee S-C			pno	Biblical
RAFFMAN, Relly Shall I compare thee to a summer's day? AMP				Shakespeare
ROBINSON, Earl In the folded and quiet yesterdays SHAW		Bar, Narr	orch(R)	Carl Sandburg
ROGERS, Bernard Dirge for two veterans TP			pno or str orch(R)	Walt Whitman
Psalm 114 TP			pno	Biblical
ROREM, Ned Letters from Paris B&H			pno or cham orch(R)	from "Paris Journal" by Janet Flanner
Spring. The French telephone. Summer. Colette. Autumn. The sex of the automobile. Winter. Mistinguett. Spring again.				
Love devine, all loves excelling B&H				Charles Wesley
A sermon on miracles B&H	unison		str orch(R)	Paul Goodman
Three incantations from a marionette tale B&H (See also "Solo Vocal")	unison			Charles Boultenhouse
Two holy songs (Psalms 134 and 150) SMPC			org or pno	Biblical

Composer, Title and Publisher	Chorus	Solos	Accompaniment	Author of Text
ROSEN, Jerome Three songs for chorus B&H Snowbird blues Good night, Mac Folk tale			pno	Edwin Honig William Van O'Connor Celeste Turner Wright
RUSSELL, John Walk this mile in silence AMP				Donald Jeffrey Hayes
SACCO, P. Peter Autumn L-G (See also "Women's Chorus")				Thomas Hood
Awake, O shepherds WIM				old Polish text
Daybreak WIM			pno	Henry Wadsworth Longfellow
Mr. Nobody WIM			pno	anon
Ring out, wild bells WIM			pno	Alfred Lord Tennyson
Seaweed WIM			pno	Henry Wadsworth Longfellow
Song of the brook WIM (See also "Women's Chorus")			pno	Alfred Lord Tennyson
Teach me, O Lord, the way of Thy statutes (Psalm 119) WIM				Biblical
SANDERS, Robert L. Chanson of the bells of Osenèy CF	SAATTBB			Cale Young Rice
SANKEY, Ira D., et al. (H. Wiley Hitchcock, Ed.) Gospel hymns nos. 1 to 6 complete (New York, 1894. The final culmination of the gospel hymnbooks produced from 1875 on.) DCP				
SCHRAMM, Harold Alarippu MCA (See also "Percussion")	speaking ch		perc	arranged from Bharata Natyam by Harold Schramm
India: a choral poem CF				adapted from verses compiled in "Folk

Voice: Mixed Chorus

Composer, Title and Publisher	Chorus	Solos	Accompaniment	Author of Text
Beat the drum. How can I tell (SSA). I will go with you. It was not my fate (TBB). O water-girl. Two love lyrics TP Separation. Rejoinment.				songs of India" by Hem Barua Harold Schramm
SHAPERO, Harold Hebrew cantata SMPC		S, A, T, B		Jehuda Halevi (1086-1140)
1. All the stars of morning			org & trp	
2. Beside an apple tree		Bar	hp	
3. Rarest beauty		Bar	hp	
4. The heritage of the Lord		S	org & fl	
5. Stars of the world			org & trp	
6. A servant of God		T	org, vln, hp	
7. Slaves of time		A	org & fl	
8. Until day and night shall cease			org & trp	
SIEGMEISTER, Elie As I was going along (from "Sing out sweet land") MCA			pno	Edward Eager
SKOLNIK, Walter Zoological studies EV The bison. The dodo. The vulture.			pno	Hilaire Belloc
SLEETH, Natalie Jazz gloria CF			3 trp, c-b, bongo dr	liturgical
SMITH, Hale In memorium - Beryl Rubenstein GAL 1. Vocalise 2. Poème d'automne 3. Elegy			pno or cham orch(R)	vocalise Langston Hughes Russell Atkins
SPIES, Claudio Animula, vagula, blandula B&H				attributed to Emperor Hadrian
SPIZIZEN, Louise Weary with toil TP				Shakespeare
STARER, Robert On the nature of things MCA				

Composer, Title and Publisher	Chorus	Solos	Accompaniment	Author of Text
1. Death is nothing to us				Lucretius; trans: James H. Mantinband
2. To everything there is a season				Biblical
3. Pain has an element of blank				Emily Dickinson
4. Sorrow				Samuel Rowley
5. A little nonsense				anon
6. Grieve not, dear love				John Digby (Earl of Bristol)
STEWART, Kensey D. Alleluia L-G				liturgical
STRILKO, Anthony Blow, northern wind TP			pno	Walter de la Mare
SUSA, Conrad David's kingly city HWG			org or cham orch(R)	Hildebert of Lavardin; trans: William Crashaw
Three mystical carols ECS				
1. The shepherds sing (Christmas)				George Herbert
2. This endrys night		A, T	org	anon (15th cent)
3. Let us gather hand in hand			org	anon (14th cent)
SYDEMAN, William Defiance of Prometheus ECS				from Aeschylus (Prometheus Bound)
TAYLOR, Clifford Melancholy L-G			pno	Marianne Daransky
Say now, ye lovely social band L-G			picc, perc, pno	trad (from collection of folk music of Western Pennsylvania by Jacob A. Evanson)
Sweet Canaan L-G				trad
TAYLOR, Priscilla Four songs WLP Song to spring. Summer soliloquy. Chant of autumn. Lullaby of winter.			pno	Priscilla Taylor

Composer, Title and Publisher	Chorus	Solos	Accompaniment	Author of Text
THOMPSON, Randall The passion according to St. Luke ECS Part I: The entry into Jerusalem. The Pass- over. The institution of the Lord's supper. The agony in the garden. Part II: Peter's denial. The mocking of Jesus; His confession. The trial. The march to Calvary. The Crucifixion. The entombment.		T, Bar	orch(R)	Biblical
A psalm of thanksgiving (a cantata) (Psalm 107) ECS	with two-part children's chorus		pno or org or orch(R)	The Book of Common Prayers and King James versions combined
Introduction: Chorale prelude, "Nun danket" 1. O give thanks unto the Lord. 2. They wandered in the wilder- ness 3. Such as sit in darkness 4. Foolish men are plagued for their of- fence 5. They that go down to the sea in ships 6. He turneth the wilder- ness into a standing water 7. Now thank we all our God				
TIRRO, Frank Sing a new song WLP				Frank Tirro
TUBB, Monte The proposal AMP				trad
VAN VACTOR, David Choruses from A Shrop- shire Lad (published separately) GAL 1. Far in a western brookland 2. Say, lad, have you things to do? 3. When I was one and twenty 4. With rue my heart is laden				A. E. Housman
VERCOE, Barry Digressions EV	SSAATTBB		orch & computer- generated sounds (R)	"Songs from the slums" by Toyohiko Kagawa

Composer, Title and Publisher	Chorus	Solos	Accompaniment	Author of Text
VIERRA, M. L. Out of the depths (Psalm 130) B&H				Biblical
WARREN, Elinor Remick Hymn of the city CF			pno or org	William Cullen Bryant
To my native land ECS				Henry Wadsworth Longfellow
WASHBURN, Robert Now welcome summer OX			pno	Robert Washburn
Summer night OX		S	pno	Robert Washburn
WEAVER, John Epiphany alleluias B&H			org	from the Propers for the Ephiphany season
Psalm 100 B&H			org	Biblical
WEINER, Lawrence A psalm of prayer and praise (Psalms 5 and 8) SHAW			org or 3 trp, 3 trb, timp	Biblical
WHEAR, Paul Psalms of celebration (Psalms nos. 47, 92, 133, 138) LMP			org or orch(R)	Biblical
Two choruses from The Seasons (cantata) LMP Summer. Winter.				Ralph Stutzman
WHITE, Donald H. Psalm LMP				Biblical
WIENHORST, Richard Hear, O Lord (Psalm 27) AMP Antiphon. Psalm. Gloria patria.				Biblical
I know the thoughts I think AMP				Biblical
O Lord, Thine enemies roar (Psalms 74 and 46) AMP				Biblical
WILLIAMS, David H. Take my life, and let it be (in Calypso style) HWG			pno	David H. Williams

Composer, Title and Publisher	Chorus	Solos	Accompaniment	Author of Text
Three Lenten scenes (a cantata) HWG The last supper. The Mount of Olives. Calvary.		S (or T), Bar	org	Biblical
WORK, John Wesley				
The singers MIL			pno or orch(R)	Henry Wadsworth Longfellow
WYTON, Alec				
Mass for St. Peter HWG Kyrie. Sanctus. Benedictus qui venit. Agnus Dei. Gloria in excelsis. Christ our Passover. Worthy art Thou.	2-part ch in any combination		org	liturgical
YARDUMIAN, Richard				
Mass ("Come, Creator spirit") EV Kyrie. Gloria. Credo. Sanctus. Agnus Dei.		T or S	orch(R)	liturgical
YORK, Walter Wynn				
A collect for peace AMP	SSATB			Book of Common Prayer
ZANINELLI, Luigi				
Autumn reverie SHAW			pno or hp	Ann Crull
Freshman dance (satirical vignette) SHAW Being at the dance. Somehow this isn't the way. Baby, set me free! Being at the dance (reprise).			instr. combo: sax, pno, c-b, dr, gtr	Luigi Zaninelli
Liturgical suite SHAW I. Holy, holy, holy II. Lamb of God III. Lord have mercy IV. Glory to God in the highest			org	liturgical
Speak up! (miniature choral opera) SHAW	SAB		pno	Luigi Zaninelli
ZIMMERMAN, Phyllis				
Alleluia AMP				liturgical

WOMEN'S CHORUS (SSA a cappella unless otherwise indicated)

Composer, Title and Publisher	Chorus	Solos	Accompaniment	Author of Text
ADLER, Samuel				
In nature's ebb and flow	SSAA		pno	
1. Spring ecstasy				Lizette Woodworth Reese
2. The dark hills				Edwin Arlington Robinson
3. The lilac				Hubert Wolfe
4. The mountains grow unnoticed				Emily Dickinson
5. God's world				Edna St. Vincent Millay
AUERBACH, Norman				
Three choral songs TP	SSAA			Walter de la Mare
The ghost. The vision. The snowflake.				
BACON, Ernst				
From Emily's diary GS	SSAA	S, m-S, A	pno	Emily Dickinson
1. Preface (piano solo) 2. My river runs to thee (air for ch) 3. I dwell in possibility (S solo) 4. A drop fell on the apple tree (S solo & ch) 5. A daisy follows soft the sun (ch) 6. What soft cherubic creatures (ch) 7. When roses cease to bloom (m-S solo) 8. It's coming - the postponeless creature (ch) 9. "Unto me?" (m-S and A duet with ch) 10. Not what we did shall be the test (ch) 11. Afterthought (piano solo)				
BAKSA, Robert F.				
Songs of late summer SHAW				from ancient Chinese poems
Falling leaves. Willows. Dawn.				
BARAB, Seymour				
First person feminine B&H			pno	Sara Teasdale
Pierrot. The daisy. The song for Colin. The wayfarer. The look. Love me. The kiss.				

Composer, Title and Publisher	Chorus	Solos	Accompaniment	Author of Text
BARBER, Samuel On the death of Antony (from Antony and Cleopatra) GS (See also "Mixed Chorus")			pno	Shakespeare
BAVICCHI, John Five short poems OX Jenny kiss'd me Let tomorrow take care of tomorrow Mister Finney What a dainty life When icicles hang by the wall (All songs available separately)	SSAA			Leigh Hunt Swain anon John Nabbes Shakespeare
BEESON, Jack Homer's woe (12 rounds for treble voices) B&H Teeth and gums. Sir Eachknight. Long song. An egg. A well. A walnut. The man, the stool, the mutton, and the dog. The one-eyed man. A thorn. An egg. Wishful thinking. A bed. (See also "Men's Chorus")			anon	
BERKOWITZ, Leonard Chamber music AMP		S	vln, vla or pno	Robert Frost
BIELAWA, Herbert The cradle L-G	SSAA			from Corner's Geistliche Nachtigal; trans: Robert Graves
BILLINGS, William Psalm 23 (Cross street) (arr: Nick Rossi) MCA			pno	Joseph Addison
BINKERD, Gordon Alleluia for St. Francis B&H (See also "Men's Chorus") The beautiful changes B&H Hope is the thing with feathers B&H	SSAA SSAA		org	from the Roman- Seraphic Missal Richard Wilbur Emily Dickinson

Composer, Title and Publisher	Chorus	Solos	Accompaniment	Author of Text
Love looks for love B&H (from Set I "To Electra"; See also "Mixed Chorus")	SSSAA			Robert Herrick
Scapulis suis AMP	SSAA			liturgical
BRIGHT, Houston				
The tale untold SHAW			pno	Percy B. Shelley
When the spring is on the meadow SHAW			pno	Houston Bright
CALDWELL, Mary E.				
Shine lovely Christmas star (from the opera, A Gift of Song) B&H			pno	Mary E. Caldwell
CARTER, John				
Three canzonets on love FM				
1. Love at first sight				Avery Giles
2. Take, o take those lips away				Shakespeare
3. Sweet, let me go				anon (17th cent)
CRESTON, Paul				
None lives forever CF			pno or org	Rabindranath Tagore
DAVIS, Katherine K.				
The lamb GAL	SA		pno	William Blake
DELLO JOIO, Norman				
Bright star (Light of the world) EBM (See also "Solo Vocal" and "Men's Chorus")	SA		pno	Norman Dello Joio
DROSTE, Doreen				
Sixpence in her shoe AMP	SA		pno	Elizabethan tale by Richard Corbet
ELLIOTT, Clinton				
The owl and the pussy-cat MCA	SSAA		pno	Edward Lear
FERGUSON, Edwin Earle				
Folk song: the stars came AMP			pno	Robert Hillyer
FINK, Michael				
From a very little sphinx ECS Come along in then. Oh, Burdock. Look, Edwin! I know a hundred ways to die. Wonder where this horseshoe went.	SSAA	S	str qrt(R) or str orch(R)	Edna St. Vincent Millay

Composer, Title and Publisher	Chorus	Solos	Accompaniment	Author of Text
FRACKENPOHL, Arthur				
Hogamus, higamus (double fugue for speaking chorus and perc) EBM (See also "Mixed Chorus", "Men's Chorus" and "Percussion")				anon
Lovers love the spring EBM (See also "Men's Chorus")			pno, gtr c-b, dr	Shakespeare
My love is come to me EBM			pno	Christina Rossetti
News items EBM			pno	compiled by Harold Helfer from New York Times Magazine
1. Delayed action	SA			
2. Not so vital statistics	SSA			
3. Collegiate champions	SA			
Odd owls EBM			pno	John Hollander
1. Scowl owl (Alfred)				
2. Howel owl (Mustapha)				
3. Vowel owl (Roger)				
Three cautionary tales EBM			pno	Hilaire Belloc
The yak. The vulture. The python (SA)				
FULLER, Jeanne Weaver				
maggie and milly and molly and may AMP	SA			e.e. cummings
GOLDSMITH, Owen				
The weather's criminal B&H Smog. Cold. Colder. Warm.			pno	Edwin Honig
GOODMAN, Joseph				
Lyrics from the Spanish AB				
1. El pavo real				Gabriela Mistral
2. Romance de la Luna, Luna				Garcia Lorca
3. El silencio				Garcia Lorca
4. Tamborilero				Carlos Blanco
GRUNDMAN, Clare				
Three noels B&H (For contents, see "Mixed Chorus")	SA		pno	trad
HOVHANESS, Alan				
Fuji, Op. 182 (a cantata) CFP			fl, hp(pno) or str orch(R)	text from Japanese

Composer, Title and Publisher	Chorus	Solos	Accompaniment	Author of Text
KORTE, Karl Aspects of love ECS (for contents and authors, see "Mixed Chorus")				
LANE, Richard Cradle song CF			pno	William Blake
MARTIRANO, Salvatore O, O, O, O, that Shake- speherian rag AMP (For contents, see "Mixed Chorus")				Shakespeare
MAYER, William Barbara - what have you done? CF (See also "Solo vocal")	SS			Susan Otto
McAFEE, Don An Elizabethan lullaby L-G	SA		pno	Richard Corbet (17th cent)
McKAY, George F. The shepherd SHAW			pno	William Blake

MURRAY, Lyn
Sleep now on thy natal
  day (from "The
  Miracle")   MCA
			pno	Norman Corwin

PINKHAM, Daniel Magnificat CFP		S	pno or 2 ob, 2 bsn, hp	liturgical
The lamb ECS	unison		pno, gtr	William Blake
POLIFRONE, Jon Three madrigals AMP I gave to love. Maiden prithee. Two little ladies. (See also "Mixed Chorus")				Helen Louise Quig
PYLE, Francis Johnson The fall CF			pno	Harold Enrico
Henry was a worthy king EV			pno	trad
A mountain tarn EV			pno	William George Russell
O love that sings CF			pno	Harold Enrico
Three amusements EV	SA			
1. Buzzy Brown				Leroy Jackson
2. Old Johnny Dades				Edward K. West
3. Off to Yakima				Leroy Jackson
READ, Gardner Nocturne AMP	SSAA	S	pno	Frances Frost

Composer, Title and Publisher	Chorus	Solos	Accompaniment	Author of Text
ROREM, Ned Prayers and responses B&H (See also "Men's Chorus")	SA			Biblical
SACCO, P. Peter Autumn WIM (See also "Mixed Chorus") Song of the brook WIM (See also "Mixed Chorus")			pno pno	Thomas Hood Alfred Lord Tennyson
SCHICKELE, Peter The last supper EV				Biblical
SKOLNIK, Walter Historical limericks (about Liszt, Haydn and Brahms) EV				anon
SMITH, Julia Enrich your life with music TP	SSAA		pno	Kathleen Lemmon
STARER, Robert Come, sleep MCA I'm nobody MCA			pno	John Fletcher Emily Dickinson
STEVENS, Halsey Psalm 98 PIC			pno	Biblical
THOMSON, Virgil Mass MCA	SA		perc ad lib	liturgical
TUBB, Monte Libera me (Free me, Lord) L-G	SA		pno	liturgical
VERNON, Knight Haiku West EV 1. Magical nature 2. Winter snow (a round) 3. The seagull 4. A tiny cell 5. Noise				 Sharon Kavisto Eric Beutter Marjorie van Atta Joy Sand Catherine Trinka
WALTON, Kenneth Hush, my love CF O lovely world of mine CF			pno pno	Elfrida Norden Evelyn Walton
WARREN, Elinor Remick From this summer garden CF			pno	Paula Romay

Composer, Title and Publisher	Chorus	Solos	Accompaniment	Author of Text
WATSON, Walter				
Five Japanese love poems GS			pno	trans: Leon Zolbrod
1. Songs of the East (from the Manyoshū, anon)				
2. from the Senzaishū (Lady Herikawa, 12th cent)				
3. from the Shinkokinshū (Sono No Yoshitada, 10th cent)				
4. from the Gosenshū (Fujiwara No Okikaze)				
5. Haiku (Oshū [a courtesan]), no dates				

MEN'S CHORUS (TTBB a cappella unless otherwise indicated)

Composer, Title and Publisher	Chorus	Solos	Accompaniment	Author of Text
BEESON, Jack				
Homer's woe (12 rounds for treble voices) B&H (For contents, see "Women's Chorus")				anon
BINKERD, Gordon				
Alleluia for St. Francis B&H (See also "Women's Chorus")			org	from the Roman-Seraphic Missal
and viva sweet love B&H	TBB		pno(4-hands)	e.e. cummings
Dum medium silentium B&H				Liber Usualis
Liebeslied B&H				Rainer Maria Rilke; trans: Ludwig Lewisohn
BLANK, Allan				
Give ear to my words, O Lord (Psalm 5) TP				Biblical
BRIGHT, Houston				
I hear a voice a-prayin' SHAW				Houston Bright
Sailor's alleluia EBM				Houston Bright
DELLO JOIO, Norman				
Bright star (Light of the world) EBM (See also "Solo Vocal" and "Women's Chorus")	TB		pno	Norman Dello Joio
FRACKENPOHL, Arthur				
Hogamus, higamus (double fugue for speaking chorus) EBM	TBB		perc	anon

Composer, Title and Publisher	Chorus	Solos	Accompaniment	Author of Text
(See also "Mixed Chorus", "Women's Chorus" and "Percussion")				
Lovers love the spring EBM	TBB		pno, gtr, dr, c-b	Shakespeare
(See also "Women's Chorus")				
FRANCO, Johan				
Seven songlets WLP			pno	
1. Little boy, full of joy...				William Blake
2. Sport that wrinkled care derides...				John Milton
3. Our hopes like towering falcons...				Matthew Prior
4. O'er the glad waters...				Lord Byron
5. On with the dance...				Lord Byron
6. From toil he wins his spirits light...				Thomas Gray
7. I heard an angel singing...				William Blake
GARLICK, Antony				
Twelve madrigals WLP				
1. Bright clouds				Edward Thomas
2. Days too short				Wm. H. Davies, alt
3. Gorse				Helen Foley
4. The happy child				Wm. H. Davies
5. I am tired of the wind				Gordon Bottomley
6. I love the beginning of all rain				Geoffrey Scott
7. In September				Francis Ledwidge
8. The moon				Wm. H. Davies
9. Northern light				L.A.G. Strong
10. Over hill, over dale				Shakespeare
11. Tall nettles				Edward Thomas
12. Tell me where is fancy bred				Shakespeare
GRUNDMAN, Clare				
Three noels B&H			pno	trad
(For contents, see "Mixed Chorus")				
HOVHANESS, Alan				
Protest and prayer CFP		T	org	Alan Hovhaness
Prelude. Hymn.				
KECHLEY, Gerald				
Psalm 150 WLP			org or 3 trp, hn, 2 trb	Biblical

Composer, Title and Publisher	Chorus	Solos	Accompaniment	Author of Text
KORTE, Karl Aspects of love ECS (For contents and authors see "Mixed Chorus")				
LATHAM, William Songs of a day Rome was not built in AMP 1. On a hairy philosopher 2. A kiss 3. A boozer's dream 4. On a statue of Venus				6th cent Latin poets of Car- thage, the first by Luxorius and the others anon
MARTIRANO, Salvatore O, O, O, O, that Shakespeherian rag AMP (For contents, see "Mixed Chorus")				Shakespeare
MONACO, Richard Four songs for literary nay-sayers JF 1. 17th century offsight 2. Through glasses darkly 3. & 4. American ditties I and II			pno	Ruth Limmer
RHEA, Raymond She walks in beauty LMP				Lord Byron
ROREM, Ned I feel death B&H Prayers and responses B&H (See also "Women's Chorus")	TBB TB			John Dryden Biblical
SACCO, P. Peter The snowstorm WIM			pno	Ralph Waldo Emerson
SOWERBY, Leo Psalms nos. 70, 124, 133 HWG (Published only separately)			org	Biblical
THOMSON, Virgil Capitals capitals B&H		male qrt: 2 T, Bar, B	pno	Gertrude Stein
Mass MCA	TB		perc ad lib	liturgical

CHORUS WITH INSTRUMENTAL ACCOMPANIMENT
(including full orchestra, chamber orchestra, string orchestra, band and smaller ensembles)

Composer, Title and Publisher	Chorus	Solos	Accompaniment	Author of Text	Duration* (min)
ADLER, Samuel Wisdom cometh with the years PIC(R)	SATB		full	Countee Cullen	4
BERKOWITZ, Leonard Chamber music	SSA	S	vln, vla	Robert Frost	8
BLAKLEY, D. Duane Jesus Christ, the Crucified (a contemporary cantata) SHAW	SATB	S, A, T, B, Narr	brass qrt and perc	Biblical and trad	NA**
BLITZSTEIN, Marc This is the garden (a cantata of New York) CHAP(R) (For contents, see "Mixed Chorus")	SATB		full	Marc Blitzstein	NA
BRIGHT, Houston Vision of Isaiah SHAW(R) (For contents, see "Mixed Chorus")	SSAATTBB		full	Biblical	12
DALLIN, Leon Songs of praise MCA(R) (For contents, see "Mixed Chorus")	SATB	A, T	full or band	Biblical	NA
DAVISON, John Lo, this land EBM(R)	SATB		full or band	Walt Whitman	3.5
DELLO JOIO, Norman Evocations EBM(R)	SATB		full		
1. Visitants at night				Robert Hillyer	16
2. Promise of spring				Richard Hovey	16
Mass EBM(R)	SATB		brass ensemble	liturgical	NA

---

*Approximate

**In a few instances, the timings in minutes were not indicated in the scores or from information received from publishers. In those cases, the symbol "NA" is used.

Composer, Title and Publisher	Chorus	Solos	Accompaniment	Author of Text	Duration (min)
Years of the modern EBM	SATB		brass and perc	Walt Whitman	15
DEL TREDICI, David Pop-Pourri B&H(R)	SATB	ampli-fied S solo (and coun-ter-tenor or m-S ad lib)	amplified solo-rock group of 2 sax and 2 electric gtr and orch	from Alice in Wonderland by Lewis Carroll and the Litany of the Blessed Virgin Mary	26
DIAMOND, David To music (choral symphony) SMPC(R) (For contents, see "Mixed Chorus")	SATB	T, B-Bar	full	John Masefield & Henry Wadsworth Longfellow	NA
DIEMER, Emma Lou Shepherd to his love EBM	SATB		fl & pno	Christopher Marlowe	3
DRAESEL, Jr. and H. Bruce Lederhouse Celebration (mass with a rock beat) CF	unison		gtr, dr	liturgical	NA
Rejoice (mass in contemporary folk style) CF	unison		gtr	liturgical	NA
DUNFORD, Benjamin The unspeakable gift (Christmas cantata) JF (For contents, see "Mixed Chorus")	SAB	Bar	3 trp, 3 trb, tba, timp, perc (4 players)	Biblical	25
Psalm 103 JF	SATB	Bar	2 hn, 3 trp, 3 trb, tba, timp, perc	Biblical	12.5
DVORAK, Robert Songs of deliverance (cantata) COL(R)	SATB	Narr	brass, str, perc	Biblical	15
FELDMAN, Morton The swallows of Salangan CFP(R)	SATB		7 vlc, 4 fl, a-fl, 5 trp, 2 tba, 2 vib, 2 pno	vocalise	NA

Composer, Title and Publisher	Chorus	Solos	Accompaniment	Author of Text	Duration (min)
Chorus and instruments (II) CFP	SATB		chimes, tba	vocalise	NA
FINK, Michael From a very little sphinx ECS(R) (For contents, see "Women's Chorus")	SSAA	S	str qrt or str orch	Edna St. Vincent Millay	6
FLAGELLO, Nicolas Te Deum for all mankind CF(R)	SATB		full	from Latin liturgy and "Laus Deo" by John Greenleaf Whittier	7
GOEMANNE, Noel Entrata (Psalm 99) WLP	SATB		3 trp, 2 trb, timp	Biblical	4
HANSON, Howard The mystic trumpeter CF(R)	SATB	Narr	full	Walt Whitman	16
Streams in the desert CF(R)	SATB		full	Biblical	12
Two Psalms (nos. 121 and 150) CF(R)	SATB		full	Biblical	9
HASLAM, Herbert Special starlight TP(R)	SATB with treble voices	Narr	full	Carl Sandburg	20
HOPSON, Hal Canticle of praise SHAW	SATB		org & 3 trp	Biblical and St. Francis of Assisi; trans: William Draper	NA
HOVHANESS, Alan Fuji (cantata) CFP(R)	SSA		fl, hp, str	Alan Hovhaness (from Japanese texts)	15
Make a joyful noise (cantata) CFP(R) (For contents, see "Mixed Chorus")	SATB		org, 2 trp, 2 trb	Biblical	12
O Lord God of Hosts CFP	SATB		2 trp, 2 trb ad lib	Biblical	5
The Lord is my Shepherd (Psalm 23) CFP	SATB		6 vln	Biblical	3.5

Composer, Title and Publisher	Chorus	Solos	Accompaniment	Author of Text	Duration (min)
HUNKINS, Eusebia					
Americana CF(R)			orch or band	Eusebia Hunkins	12
IVES, Charles					
Circus band PIC(R)	SATB		cham	Charles Ives	NA
JARRETT, Jack					
Chorale symphony on American poems (CF(R) (For contents and authors of texts, see "Mixed Chorus")	SATB		orch or band		16.5
JONES, Robert W.					
Hist whist SHAW	SATB choric speech		b-dr, sn-dr, tri, cmb	e.e. cummings	3
Magnificat and nunc dimittis HWG	SATB		3 trp, 3 trb, timp, org	liturgical	10
KECHLEY, Gerald					
"The dwelling of youth" CF(R)	SATB		band	Gerald Kechley after ancient Sanskrit	9
Psalm 150 WLP	TTBB		3 trp, hn, 2 trb	Biblical	6
KING, Alvin					
Psalm 47 ("O clap your hands, all ye people") AUG	SATB	Narr	4 trp, 2 trb, hn, tba	Biblical	8
KIRK, Theron					
O sons and daughters JF	SATB		org, trp, tba, timp	a French carol; trans: J.M. Neale	2.5
Rejoice in the Lord (Psalm 33) EBM	SATB		org, 2 trp	Biblical	2.5
Sing for joy EBM	SATB		pno and org, opt: 2 trp, 2 trb	Biblical	2.5
KLEINSINGER, George					
I hear America singing (a cantata) EBM(R) (For contents, see "Mixed Chorus")	SATB	Bar	full	Walt Whitman	30

Composer, Title and Publisher	Chorus	Solos	Accompaniment	Author of Text	Duration (min)
KNEALE, Peter Lute book lullaby MCA	SATB		gtr	William Ballet (17th cent)	NA
KUBIK, Gail A Christmas set MCA(R) (For contents and authors, see "Mixed Chorus")	SATB		cham		30
LADERMAN, Ezra The trials of Galileo (oratorio) OX(R)	SATB	A, 2T, counter-tenor, 2 Bar, B	full	Joe Darion	90
LOJEWSKI, Harry V. Mass: Americana WLP (For contents, see "Mixed Chorus")	SATB		org & gtr	Bishops' Committee on the Liturgy	NA
LO PRESTI, Ronald Alleluia! Christus natus est CF	SATB		brass ensemble	liturgical	4.5
MAILMAN, Martin Concord hymn MIL	SATB		hp (or pno or gtr)	Ralph Waldo Emerson	3
MARTIRANO, Salvatore O, O, O, O, that Shakespeherian rag (For contents, see "Mixed Chorus") AMP(R)	SATB		cl, sax, trp, trb, c-b, pno, perc	Shakespeare	20
MAYER, William Letters home MCA(R)	SATB	m-S, T	full	consists largely of authentic letters from soldiers fighting in Vietnam	8
MECHEM, Kirke The ballad of Befana (an Epiphany legend) ECS	SATB		gtr	Phyllis McGinley	NA
Christmas carol ECS	SATB		gtr	Sara Teasdale	NA

Composer, Title and Publisher	Chorus	Solos	Accompaniment	Author of Text	Duration (min)
MOEVS, Robert					
A brief mass for the new church EBM(R)	SSAT		cham	liturgical	NA
PERSICHETTI, Vincent					
The creation (oratorio) EV(R) (For contents, see "Mixed Chorus")	SATB	S, A, T, B	full	based on texts from mythological, scientific, poetic and Biblical sources	60
The Pleiades EV(R)	SATB		trp & str or trp & org or trp & pno	Walt Whitman	23
PINKHAM, Daniel					
The lamb ECS	SSA (unison)		pno, gtr	William Blake	2.5
Magnificat CFP	SSA	S	2 ob, 2 bsn, hp	liturgical	5
Prelude, adagio and chorale CFP	unison		2 trp, hn, trb, tba	Daniel Pinkham	NA
Psalm set CFP (For contents, see "Mixed Chorus")	SATB		2 trp, 2 trb	Biblical	NA
Sometimes the soul ECS	SATB		pno, gtr	Norma Farber	2.5
ROBINSON, Earl					
In the folded and quiet yesterdays SHAW(R)	SATB	Bar, Narr	full	Carl Sandburg	9
ROGERS, Bernard					
Dirge for two veterans TP(R)			str	Walt Whitman	NA
ROREM, Ned					
Letters from Paris B&H(R) (For contents, see "Mixed Chorus")	SATB		cham	from "Paris Journal" by Janet Flanner	25
A sermon on miracles B&H(R)	unison with a solo voice		str	Paul Goodman	6.5
SHAPERO, Harold					
Hebrew cantata SMPC (For contents, see "Mixed Chorus")	SATB	S, A, T, B	hp, fl, trp, vln	Jehuda Halevi (1086-1140)	27

Composer, Title and Publisher	Chorus	Solos	Accompaniment	Author of Text	Duration (min)
SLEETH, Natalie Jazz gloria CF	SATB		3 trp, c-b, bongo dr	liturgical	3.5
SMITH, Hale In memorium - Beryl Rubenstein GAL(R) (For contents, see "Mixed Chorus")	SATB		cham	Langston Hughes and Russell Adkins	10.5
SUSA, Conrad David's kingly city HWG(R)	SATB		cham	Hildebert of Lavardin; trans: William Crashaw	NA
TAYLOR, Clifford Say now, ye lovely social band L-G	SATB		picc, perc, pno	from collection of folk music of Western Pennsylvania by Jacob A. Evanson	NA
THOMPSON, Randall The passion according to St. Luke ECS(R) (For contents, see "Mixed Chorus")	SATB	T, Bar	full	Biblical	92
A psalm of thanksgiving (a cantata) (Psalm 107) ECS(R) (For contents, see "Mixed Chorus")	SATB and two-part children's chorus		full	The Book of Common Prayer and King James versions combined	50
VERCOE, Barry Digressions EV(R)	SSAATTBB		full & computer-generated sounds	from "Songs from the slums" by Toyohiko Kagawa	15
WEINER, Lawrence A psalm of prayer and praise (Psalms 5 & 8) SHAW	SATB		3 trp, 3 trb, timp	Biblical	5
WHEAR, Paul Psalms of celebration (nos. 47, 92, 133, 138) LMP(R)	SATB		full	Biblical	16

Composer, Title and Publisher	Chorus	Solos	Accompani- ment	Author of Text	Dura- tion (min)
WORK, John Wesley The singers MIL(R)	SATB	Bar	full	Henry Wads- worth Longfellow	15
YARDUMIAN, Richard Mass ("Come, Creator spirit") EV(R) (For contents, see "Mixed Chorus")	SATB	T or S	full	liturgical	42
ZANINELLI, Luigi Freshman dance (satirical vi- gnette) SHAW (For contents, see "Mixed Chorus")	SATB		instr. combo: sax, pno, c-b, dr, gtr	Luigi Zaninelli	10

2. INSTRUMENTAL SOLO

KEYBOARD MUSIC

PIANO, TWO HANDS (Including harpsichord)

ABRAMSON, Robert
Dance variations   GEN

AITKEN, Hugh
Piano fantasy in 2 movements OX
Three connected pieces: thirds,
melody and fifths   OX

ALLANBROOK, Douglas
40 changes   B&H

ANTHEIL, George
Piano pastels   WEIN

BABIN, Stanley
Four piano studies   WME
Sonatina No. 1 and No. 2   MCA
Three piano pieces   MCA
Musette. Fugue. Presto.

BEESON, Jack
Fifth sonata   TP

BERNSTEIN, Seymour
Toccata Française   CF

BINKERD, Gordon
Concert set for piano   B&H
Entertainments for piano B&H
Brief encounter. The trumpet,
the tuba and the metronone.
Nearer than hands and feet.
Rain. Tristan and the magic
broomstick. Being beauteous.
Graceful exit.
Piano miscellany   B&H
Lake lonely. Rough-and-
tumble. Something serious.
For the Union dead. Country
dance.
Sonata   B&H

BOLCOM, William
12 etudes for piano   TP

BRUBECK, Dave
Jazz impressions of New York
EBM

CRESTON, Paul
Rhythmicon, book 5   COL

CRIST, Bainbridge
Fantasie in D-major   OX

CROLEY, Randell
Quattro espressioni   JBI

CUSTER, Arthur
Four ideas for piano   GEN

DELLO JOIO, Norman
Capriccio (on the interval of a
second)   EBM

DEL TREDICI, David
Fantasy pieces   B&H

DIAMOND, David
Gambit   SMPC
8 piano pieces   GS

DIEMENTE, Edward
Clavier sonata   WLP
Four waltzes   WLP
In a call of wind   WLP

ELWELL, Herbert
Tarantella   CF

ETLER, Alvin
Sonatina   AB

FINNEY, Ross Lee
32 piano games   CFP

FOSS, Lukas
Grotesque dance   CF
Prelude   HAR

FRACKENPOHL, Arthur
3 miniatures   EV

FRANCO, Johan
Toccata   RBB

FULEIHAN, Anis
Cypriana   SMPC
Cafe dancer. The girl from
Paphos. Kyrenia. Serenade.
Syrtôs.
(All above available only
separately)
Sonata No. 11   B&H
Sonata No. 12   B&H

GOTTSCHALK, Lous Moreau
The piano works of Louis Moreau
Gottschalk Arno Press
(Complete in 5 volumes, including photo-offset reproduc-
tions of first publication copies
[when available] or very early
printings of the 112 compositions.)

GOULD, Morton
Prelude and toccata   MIL

GUTCHE, Gene
Sonata, Op. 6, No. 3   GAL
Sonatas, Op. 32, Nos. 1 and 2
GAL

HARTLEY, Walter S.
Sonata No. 2   TP

HAUFRECHT, Herbert
Toccata on familiar tunes   AMP

HITCHCOCK, H. Wiley (Ed.)
Keyboard music of the second
New England school   DCP
(works for piano and organ by
John Knowles Paine, Arthur
Foote, and Horatio Parker.)

HOVHANESS, Alan
Farewell to the mountains   CFP
Mountain idylls   AMP

HUSTON, Scott
Penta-tholoi   GEN

JOHANNESEN, Grant
Improvisation on a Morman hymn
("Come, come, ye saints") OX

JOHNSON, Robert S.
Sonata No. 1   OX

KATZ, Erich
Six inventions (studies in modern
rhythm)   SF

KOCH, John
Suite for piano   GEN
Impromptu. Andante and
scherzo. Finale gaudioso.
(all above available only
separately.)

KRAEHENBUEHL, David
Elegy   S-B
Notturno   S-B

KRAFT, Leo
Partita   GEN
Prelude. Capriccio. Arietta.
Toccata.

KUPFERMAN, Meyer
4 pieces for piano   GEN
Short suite   GEN
Prelude. Close-up. March.
Canvas. Game.

LA MONTAINE, John
Sonata for piano   CF

LEES, Benjamin
Three preludes   B&H

LESSARD, John
Perpetual motion   GEN

MacDOWELL, Edward
Barcarolle, Op. 18, No. 1 GS
Czardas, Op. 24, No. 4   GS
Hungarian dance, Op. 39, No. 12
CF
Piano music (H. Wiley Hitchcock,
Ed.)   DCP
(including the best settings of
character pieces for piano, in-
cluding Woodland Sketches, Sea
Pieces and Fireside Tales.)
Shadow dance, Op. 39, No. 8 CF

MECHEM, Kirke
Sonata No. 1, Op. 26   ECS
Suite, Op. 5   ECS

MIDDLETON, Robert
Notebooks of designs   EBM

MUCZYNSKI, Robert
Diversions   GS
Second sonata, Op. 22   GS

PYLE, Francis Johnson
Sonata No. 2 (for free-bass ac-
cordion, piano or harpsichord)
S-C
Suite for puppeteers   S-C
Curtain! Medieval song.
Eccentric dance.

RAMEY, Phillip
Epigrams   B&H

RAPHLING, Sam
Seven mobiles   GEN
Suite (with perc)   BI
(See also "Percussion")
Two essays   GEN
I: Prelude. Serenade. Badinage.
II: Andante. Elusive waltz.
Scherzando.

ROGERS, William Keith
6 short preludes on a tone
row   AMP

ROREM, Ned
Spiders (for harpsichord) B&H

RUBENSTEIN, Beryl
Whirligig   OX

SCHIFRIN, Lalo
Mima (progressive jazz suite)
EDM

SCHRAMM, Harold
Natyamalika   GEN
1. Jatisvaram (toccata)
2. Padam (adagio)
3. Varnam (etude)
Vertical construction   GEN

SESSIONS, Roger
March   CF
Scherzino   CF

SHARAF, Frederic
Episode   CF

SHAW, Arnold
Stabiles   EBM

SMITH, Julia
Characteristic suite   TP

Canon. Waltz. Passacaglia.
March. Toccata.
Episodic suite   TP
Yellow and blue. Nocturne.
Waltz. March. Toccata.

SOWERBY, Leo
Dialog (with organ)   HWG

STEVENS, Halsey
Five Swedish folk tunes   HME

SUDERBURG, Robert
Six moments for piano   TP

WARD-STEINMAN, David
Elegy for Martin Luther King, Jr.
GAL
Three lyric preludes   GAL

WEISGALL, Hugo
Graven images No. 6   TP
Two improvisations   TP

WUORINEN, Charles
Sonata   CFP

ZABRAK, Harold
Scherzo ("Hommage à Proko-
fieff")   B&H

PIANO, FOUR HANDS
(*one piano; all others 2 pianos)

ARGENTO, Dominick
Divertimento   B&H

BROWN, Earle
Corroboree   AMP
(for three or two pianos)

COPLAND, Aaron
Dance of the adolescent (from
"Dance Symphony")   B&H
Danza de Jalisco   B&H

GOULD, Morton
Pavanne   MIL
(for 1 pno, 4-hands or for
2 pno, 4-hands)
Rumbolero   CF

HELPS, Robert
*Saccade   CFP

SPIEGELMAN, Joel
*Morsels ("Kousochki") MCA

WUORINEN, Charles
*Making ends meet   CFP

ORGAN

ALBRIGHT, William
Juba for organ   EV
Pneuma   EV

ARNATT, Ronald
Three plainsong preludes HWG
Variations on a theme by Leo
Sowerby   HWG

BARTOW, Nevett
Three early American hymn
tunes (a service sonata) SHAW
I. Prelude (based on an early
American melody)
II. Offertory (based on the
hymn tune "Avon")
III. Postlude (based on a
Southern hymn tune)
Toccata, chorale and fugue SHAW

BERLINSKI, Herman
Sinfonia No. 3 (sounds and
motions)   HWG

BINGHAM, Seth
Annunciation   HWG
Thirty-six hymn and carol canons
in free style   HWG

BINKERD, Gordon
Organ service   B&H
Prelude. Offertory. Postlude.
Studenten-Schmaus (with double
brass choir)   B&H

BROWN, Rayner
Organ sonata for two players WIM
Sonatina No. 22   WIM

CHIHARA, Paul
Prelude and motet   WIM

COPLEY, R. Evan
Eleven chorale preludes   ABP
Three chorale preludes   ABP
Three preludes and fugues ABP
Toccata   ABP

COX, Ainslee
Prelude   TP

DIEMENTE, Edward
Three versets on the theme
"Pange lingua"   WLP
Two preludes   WLP

DIEMER, Emma Lou
Fantasy on "O sacred head" B&H
He leadeth me (hymn setting
for organ)   OX
7 hymn preludes   FLAM

DORAN, Matt
Pastorale   WIM

EARLS, Paul
Huguenot fantasy   ECS
Nun danket variations   ECS

ELMORE, Robert
Concerto for brass, organ and percus-
sion HWG (see also "Percussion")
Fanfare for Easter (with trumpet,
trombone, percussion)   FLAM
Three miniatures   FLAM

FERRIS, William
Soliloquy   HWG

FINNEY, Ross Lee
Five organ fantasies   CFP
1. Advice which the hours of
darkness give
2. So long as the mind keeps
silent
3. Each answer hides future
questions
4. The leaves on the trees spoke
5. There are no summits without abysses

FOSS, Lukas
Etudes   CF

GARLICK, Antony
Ten preludes   WLP
Three fragments   WLP
Preamble. Voluntary. Toccata.

GOODE, Jack C.
Magnificat   ABP
Processional   ABP

GOODMAN, Joseph
Three preludes on Gregorian
chants   TP

HAYES, William
Sonata in D   CPH

HEMMER, Eugene
Processional and recessional
(with trumpet)   WLP

HITCHCOCK, H. Wiley (Ed.)
Keyboard music of the second
New England school   DCP
(works for piano and organ by
John Knowles Paine, Arthur
Foote and Horatio Parker)

HOPKINS, James
Adagio for organ   WLP
Five variations on "Christ lag in
Todesbanden"   WLP
(first variation also arranged
for 2 trumpets)

HOVHANESS, Alan
Sanahin (partita)   CFP

HUSTON, Scott
Diorama   GEN

JENKINS, Joseph W.
Six pieces for organ   WLP
Adagio in Phrygian modes.
Arioso. Deo gratias. Rondo.
Sonata. Upon an old English
hymn tune.

JOHNS, Donald
Triptych on Aberystwyth   WIM

JONES, Robert W.
Sonata for worship, No. 2
(for manuals alone)   SHAW

JOHNSON, David
Trumpet tune (in: Album of
Postludes)   OX

JORDAHL, Robert
Festive prelude on "O for a
thousand tongues to sing"   HWG

KOCH, Frederick
Improvisation   GEN
Two choral preludes   GEN

KUBIK, Gail
Prayer and toccata   MCA

LAZAROF, Henri
Largo   WIM

LYNN, George
Adagio   TP
Prelude and 7 brief statements   TP

MADER, Clarence
Dialogue   WIM

OCHSE, Orpha
Chaconne   WIM

PILLIN, Boris
Fugue   WIM

PINKHAM, Daniel
A prophecy   ECS

POWELL, Robert J.
Introduction and passacaglia   ABP

PURVIS, Richard
An American organ mass   FLAM
Four dubious conceits   SHAW
Organ music from Grace
Cathedral   SMP
Cortège. Novelette I, II, III.
Undulato.
Toccata marina. A retrospec-
tion.
Three fanciful concepts   SHAW

READ, Gardner
Elegiac aria   JF

ROBERTS, Myron J.
Dialogue (in: Modern Organ Music
Book 2)   OX
Pastorale and aviary   HWG

ROHLIG, Harald
Fifteen preludes   ABP
Organ prelude on "In dulci jubilo"
ABP
Sonata 1   ABP
Ten pieces for organ   ABP

ROTH, Robert N.
Improvisation on "The infant
King"   HWG

SCHMIDT, William
Chamber concerto for organ and
brass quintet   WIM
Phantasy on an American
spiritual   WIM
Sinfonia (AGO prelude book)   WIM
Two white spirituals   WIM

SMITH, Julia
Prelude in D-flat   TP

SOWERBY, Leo
  Dialog (with piano) HWG

SPONG, Jon (Arr.)
  Early American compositions for
    organ of the 18th and 19th
    centuries   ABP
  Atwell, Richard: Christmas suite
  Billings, William: Christmas
    voluntary
  Bremner, James: Trumpet air
  Carr, Benjamin: Aria
  Hewitt, James: Quiet verses for
    Holy communion
  Mason, Lowell: A joyous
    voluntary
  Read, Daniel: Trumpet tunes
    for Advent
  Whiting, George: Improvisation
    on a Bach theme

STARER, Robert
  Prelude   L-G

STOUT, Alan
  Eight organ chorales   AUG

THOMPSON, Randall
  Twenty-four preludes, four in-
    ventions and a fugue   ECS

TIRRO, Frank
  Church sonata   WLP
  Melismas for carillon or organ
    WLP

VERRALL, John
  Canzona   CFP

WAGNER, Joseph
  Liturgy   SMPC

WEATHERS, Keith
  Prelude and fugue on "Christ
    is risen"   WIM

WEAVER, John
  Toccata   B&H

WHITE, Louie L.
  Sonata for organ   HWG

WOLFORD, Darwin
  Nine psalms for organ JF

WOOLLEN, Russell
  Postlude on the solemn "Ite" WLP

WUENSCH, Gerhard
  Aria WIM
  Sonata breve   WIM
  Toccata piccola   WIM

WYTON, Alec
  Dialogue   TP

YOUNG, Gordon
  Collage for organ   FLAM
    Fanfare on "Austrian hymn";
    march on "martydom"; passa-
    caglia and fugato; postlude on
    "In Babilone"; postlude on "Lasst
    uns Erfreuen"; prelude on "St.
    Agnes"; toccata for a joyous
    occasion.
  Eight compositions for organ ABP
    Festivals. Chanson religieuse.
    Canzona. Pageant. Prelude. A
    morning prelude. Requiescat in
    pace. Prelude sombre.
  Nine pieces for organ   OX
    Air. Carillon. Chanson. Chant.
    Introitus. Modal sequence.
    Musette. Paean. Recessional.
  Nine pieces for organ   SMP
    Prelude in classic style. Pastel.
    Ricercare on "St. Anne". Psalm.
    Postludium. Toccata. Lied.
    Holiday. Spinning song.
  Organ solos for the worship
    service and recital   SHAW
    Passacaglia. Soliloquy. Scenes
    from the Holy Grail. Toccata in
    style of Scarlatti. Three anti-
    phons. Solemn prelude. Le cou-
    cou. Sonata in A-minor. The
    mysterious fountain.
  Three liturgical preludes   ABP
  Triptych   OX
    Praeludium. Lied. Toccata.
  Variations on an American hymn
    tune   JF

YOUNG, Michael E.
  Prelude and fugue   WIM
  Prelude and fugue No. 2 WIM

ACCORDIAN

LOCKWOOD, Normand
  Sonata-fantasia   OPB

SIEGMEISTER, Elie
  Improvisation, ballad and dance
    SF

CARILLON

HOVHANESS, Alan
Gamelan and Jhala   CFP

PINKHAM, Daniel
A song for the bells   CFP

STRING MUSIC
(with piano unless otherwise indicated)

VIOLIN

ADLER, Samuel
Sonata No. 2 (with pno or hpcd) OX

AITKEN, Hugh
Partita (unacc)   OX

BEESON, Jack
Sonata   TP

COWELL, Henry
Set of five (with pno and perc) CFP

DOLIN, Samuel
Sonata   AMP

HUSTON, Scott
Sonata: Venus and Mercury GEN

IVES, Charles
Largo   PIC

KOUTZEN, Doris
Music for violin alone   GEN

LEWIS, Robert Hall
Toccata (with perc) AB
(See also "Percussion")

PARRIS, Robert
Sonata (unacc) SMPC

PERLMAN, George
Elegy and habañera   TP

PLESKOW, Raoul
Bagatelles (unacc) MM

SCHICKELE, Peter
Tombeau de P.D.Q. Bach EV

SCHMIDT, William
Variations on a folk hymn
"Mississippi" WIM

SIEGMEISTER, Elie
Song for a quiet evening   MCA

SIMONDS, Bruce
Habañera   OX

TRAVIS, Roy
Duo concertante   UCP
(The rhythms of movements I
(Gakpa) and V (Asafo) have been
adapted from two Ewe dances as
noted by the composer under the
guidance of Mr. Robert Ayitee,
Chief Master Drummer of
Ghana, at the Institute of Ethno-
musicology, Univ. of Calif., Los
Angeles.)

VIOLA

ADLER, Samuel
Song and dance   OX

EFFINGER, Cecil
Melody (or for cl and pno)   TP

FULEIHAN, Anis
Recitative and scilienne   SMPC

GHENT, Emmanuel
Entelechy OX

HAUFRECHT, Herbert
Caprice (or for cl and pno) B&H

MAURY, Lowndes
Song without words WIM

MIDDLETON, Robert
Approximations   EBM

OTT, Joseph
Sonata   CBP

SACCO, P. Peter
Sequence: recitative, aria,
scherzo, eulogy   WIM

SPIES, Claudio
Viopiacem (with pno and hpcd) B&H

STEVENS, Halsey
Suite   PIC

CELLO

BINKERD, Gordon
Nocturne (with acc of mixed
voices) B&H
(See also "Mixed Chorus")
Sonata B&H

BROWN, Rayner
Sonata (with org) WIM

HEIDEN, Bernhard
Siena AB
Sonata AB

PERSICHETTI, Vincent
Sonata (unacc) EV

SCHUBEL, Max
Omphaloskepsis (unacc) OX

SIEGMEISTER, Elie
Fantasy and soliloquy (unacc) MCA

STEVENS, Halsey
Music for Christopher PIC

WEBER, Ben
Two dances (unacc) TP

GUITAR

BODA, John
Quatres etudes Byzantines TP

HARRIS, Albert
Sonatina TP

HAUFRECHT, Herbert
Hora SMPC
Waltz SMPC

PILLIN, Boris
Sonatina WIM

DOUBLE BASS

AITKEN, Hugh
Suite (unacc) OX

FREDRICKSON, Thomas
Music for double bass alone TP

RUSSELL, Armand
Buffo set GS
Chaconne GS
Solemn suite and solemn sonata
BI

SYDEMAN, William
Duo (with xy) CFP

WHITTENBERG, Charles
Conversations (unacc) CFP

HARP

CHOU, Wen-Chung
2 Chinese folk songs CFP

CRESTON, Paul
Olympia - rhapsody for harp
solo GS

DELLO JOIO, Norman
Bagatelles B&H

HUSTON, Scott
Suite of three GS

RASKIN, David
The psalmist WIM

SCHULLER, Gunther
Fantasy AMP

VAUGHAN, Clifford
Revery WIM

WOODWIND MUSIC
(with piano unless otherwise
indicated)

FLUTE

ALEXANDER, Joseph
Melody for flute GEN

BASKA, Robert F.
Aria da capo SHAW

BROWN, Rayner
Sonatina (3 contemporary unacc
solos) WIM

DI DOMINICO, Robert
Sonata   EM
Variations on a tonal theme
(unacc)   EM

DILLON, Robert
Petite etude   B&H

DORAN, Matt
Poem   WIM

EVANS, Billy G.
Caprice   SHAW

FORTNER, Jack
Cantilenae   EV

FROCK, George
Variations for multiple percussion
and flute   SMC   (See also
"Percussion")

GLASS, Philip
Serenade (unacc)   EV

HAIGH, Morris
Serenade   TP

KANTOR, Joseph
Dialogue   WIM

LADERMAN, Ezra
Sonata   OX

LANE, Richard
Sonata   CF

La VIOLETTE, Wesley
Sonata   TP

LUENING, Otto
Suite for flute alone No. 1   GAL
Pastoral prologue. Monologue.
Pastoral epilogue.

MAURY, Lowndes
Lament (3 contemporary unacc
solos)   WIM
Reflection   WIM

MAXWELL, Everett
Voice in the wilderness (3 contemporary unacc solos)   WIM

MICHALSKY, Donal R.
Partita piccolo   WIM
Prelude. Toccata. Variazioni.
Giga alla rondo.

Sonata piccolo   WIM

MOORE, James L.
Soliloquy and scherzo (with cel
and perc)   LMP
(See also "Percussion")

MUCZYNSKI, Robert
Three preludes (unacc)   GS

RAPHLING, Sam
Playthings of the wind (unacc) EM

RUSSELL, Robert
Pan, Op. 26   GEN

RYNEARSON, Paul
Eleven contemporary flute etudes
WIM

SACCO, P. Peter
Adagietto and allegro (unacc) WIM

SCHMIDT, William
Septigrams (with pno and perc)
WIM
Introduction. Quartal blues.
Syncophrases. Polyjazz. Impro-
visatorial variant. The percus-
sive rondo. Finale.
(See also "Percussion")
Variations   WIM

SIEGMEISTER, Elie
Nocturne (or ob)   MCA

SKOLNIK, Walter
Sonatina   EM

SMITH, Hale
Three brevities (unacc)   EBM

TEMPLAR, Joan
Sonnet   KMI

OBOE

BAVICCHI, John
Sonatina   OX

DILLON, Robert
Scherzo   B&H

McCLELLAN, Randall
Arioso   WIM

ODEGARD, Peter S.
Sonatina   MM

PINKHAM, Daniel
Variations (with org)   CFP

REED, Alfred
Concertino   CF

SIEGMEISTER, Elie
Nocturne (or fl)   MCA

SPENCER, Williametta
Adagio and rondo   WIM

STRILKO, Anthony
Music for oboe alone   TP

SYDEMAN, William
Variations (with hpcd)   ECS

ENGLISH HORN

STEVENS, Halsey
Three Hungarian folk songs (or
cl)   GAL

CLARINET

AITKEN, Hugh
Suite for clarinet   EV

BAVICCHI, John
Sonata (unacc)   OX

BURGE, David
Sources III (with perc)   AB
(See also "Percussion")

CAMPO, Frank
"Kinesis"   WIM

DONATO, Anthony
Sonata   SMPC

EFFINGER, Cecil
Dialogue   TP
Melody (or vla)   TP

HAUFRECHT, Herbert
Caprice (or vla)   B&H

KUPFERMAN, Meyer
Five singles (unacc)   GEN

Prelude. Cycles. Suspensions.
Toccata. Equations.

LADERMAN, Ezra
Sonata   OX

MAURY, Lowndes
Song without words   WIM

MAYER, William
Two moods (unacc)   TP

McKAY, George F.
Sonatina   WIM

McGINNIS, Donald E. and Edmund
J. Siennicki
Etudes for the advanced clarinetist
SHAW

PILLIN, Boris
Sonata   WIM

PRESSER, William
Partita (unacc)   TP

PYLE, Francis Johnson
Sonata for three (with percussion)
LPI (See also "Percussion")
Sonata: from the middle border
WIM

RARIG, John
Introduction and march   WIM

READ, Gardner
Intermezzo   CF

RICHENS, James M.
Prelude and dance   KMI

RUGOLO, Pete
Petite suite   WIM
Modella. Fugetta. Octavia.
Moderata. Conta. Waltzina.

SACCO, P. Peter
Adagietto (unacc)   WIM

SCHMIDT, William
Rhapsody No. 1   WIM
Sonatina   WIM
Variations   WIM

SIEGMEISTER, Elie
Prelude   MCA

SKOLNIK, Walter
  Intermezzo (from the clarinet
  concerto) EM

SMITH, William O.
  Five pieces for clarinet (unacc) TP

STEVENS, Halsey
  Three Hungarian folk songs (or
  E-hn) GAL

SYDEMAN, William
  Duo for B-flat clarinet PIC

TALMA, Louise
  Three dialogues EM

VAZZANA, Anthony
  Two pieces for clarinet WIM

WHITTENBERG, Charles
  Three pieces (unacc) MM

SAXOPHONE

ANDERSON, Garland
  Sonata SMC

BASSETT, Leslie
  Music for saxophone and piano CFP

BENNETT, David
  Saxophone royal SMC
  (See also "Band")

BRINDEL, Bernard
  Suite TP

CROLEY, Randell
  Partita JBI

DI DOMENICO, Robert
  Sonata MJQ

EFFINGER, Cecil
  Solitude TP

KUPFERMAN, Meyer
  In two bits GEN
  Seven inversions (unacc) GEN

KYNASTON, Trent
  Dance suite WIM

MORITZ, Edvard
  Intermezzo SMC
  Sonata SMC

MORRISSEY, John J.
  Nightfall EBM

RAPHLING, Sam
  Sonata No. 2 GEN

RAYMOND, Lewis
  Design (or for trp or hn) WIM

REED, Alfred
  Ballade SMC

SCALTER, James
  Suite (unacc) TP
  Prelude. Song. Dance.

SCHMIDT, William
  A little midnight music WIM
  Sonatina WIM

SCHMUTZ, Albert D.
  Sonata SMPC

SIEGMEISTER, Elie
  Downriver MCA

STEIN, Leon
  Sonata SMC

TURKIN, Marshall W.
  Sonata TP

TUTHILL, Burnet C.
  Sonata SMC

BASSOON

AITKEN, Hugh
  Montages (partita for solo
  bassoon) OX

CUSTER, Arthur
  Divertimento MCA

DILLON, Robert
  Lament B&H

LUENING, Otto
  Sonata GAL

SCHMIDT, William
  Phantasy WIM

SIEGMEISTER, Elie
  Contrasts MCA

WILDER, Alec
Sonata No. 2   SMC

RECORDER

KUPFERMAN, Meyer
Music from "Hallelujah the hills"
(with hpcd) GEN
Romanza. Scherzetto. Baroque
fantasy. Divertimento. Rococo
air. Valse de neige. Variations.

MILLER, Edward
Song for recorder   MM

PERSICHETTI, Vincent
Little recorder book (treble) EV

PINKHAM, Daniel
Duet (with hpcd)   ECS

STEVENS, Halsey
Sonatina piacevole (with pno or
hpcd)   PIC

TOWNSEND, Douglas
Dance- improvisation and fugue
CFP

BRASS MUSIC
(with piano unless otherwise indicated)

TRUMPET OR CORNET

BRICCETTI, Thomas A.
Sonata   MM

CHANCE, John Barnes
Credo   B&H

GOULD, Elizabeth
Andante   EV
(See also "String or Chamber
Orchestra with Solo Instru-
ment")

HARTLEY, Walter S.
Concertino   JBI
(See also "Band")

HOVHANESS, Alan
Haroutiun (Ressurection) CFP

Aria and fugue
(See also "String or Chamber
Orchestra with Solo Instrument")

KUPFERMAN, Meyer
Infinities twenty-two   GEN
Ritual. Mode. Projectile. Turn-
about. Jazz-bond.
Three ideas   GEN

PRESSER, William
Suite   KMI
Tango. Waltz. March. Scherzo.
Jig.

RAYMOND, Lewis
Design (or cor, hn, or sax) WIM

RUSSELL, Robert
Sonatina, Op. 23   GEN

SCHMIDT, William
The Turkish lady   WIM

SYDEMAN, William
The affections (7 pieces for
trumpet and piano) AMP

WEAST, Robert
Sonata   KMI

WHITTENBERG, Charles
Polyphony (unacc)   MM

FRENCH HORN

FAITH, Richard
Movements   SHAW

HADDAD, Don
Adagio and allegro   SHAW
(See also "Band")
Allegro giocoso   SHAW

KLEIN, John
A French waltz   EV

PRESSER, William
Three pieces (unacc)   JBI

RAYMOND, Lewis
Design (or trp or sax) WIM

REYNOLDS, Verne
Partita   KING

ROSENTHAL, Irving
Partita (unacc)   WIM
Prelude. Air. Bouree. Gigue.

TROMBONE

ALEXANDER, Joseph
Requiem and coda   GEN

BASSETT, Leslie
Suite (unacc)   JBI

COOLIDGE, Richard
Arioso   JBI

CROLEY, Randell
Mies structure No. 3 (unacc) JBI
Variazioni piccolo (unacc)   JBI

DUCKWORTH, William
Statements and interludes   TP

KELLY, Robert
Sonata   TP

MITSUOKA, I.
Two moments   JBI

MONACO, Richard A.
Sonata   JBI

OTT, Joseph
Toccata   CBP

PRESSER, William
Partita (unacc)   JBI
Rondo   TP
Sonatine   TP

RAHN, John
Progressive etude (unacc)   JBI

RIVARD, William H.
Sonata   TP

ROSS, Walter
Cryptical triptych   B&H

SPEARS, Jared
Recitative   JBI

STEVENS, Halsey
Sonata   PIC

STOUT, Alan
Proclamation (unacc)   JBI

TREVARTHEN, Richard
Sonata   JBI

UBER, David
Sonata   SMPC

WHEAR, Paul
Sonata   KING

WHITE, Donald H.
Sonata   SMC

YOSHIOKA, Emmett
Extase   JBI

TUBA

BROWN, Rayner
Diptych   WIM

CROLEY, Randell
3 expressioni   JBI
Variazioni (unacc)   WIM

HARTLEY, Walter S.
Aria   EV

JENNE, Glenn
Rondo   TP

KNOX, Charles
Solo for tuba (with brass trio:
trp, hn, trb)   TP

LLOYD, Gerald
Three sketches   TP

PRESSER, William
Minute sketches   JBI

SACCO, P. Peter
Fantasy   WIM
Tuba mirum (unacc)   WIM

SEAR, Walter
Sonata (unacc)   WIM

SIBBING, Robert
Sonata   TP

3. INSTRUMENTAL ENSEMBLES

STRING ENSEMBLES

DUOS AND TRIOS

BINKERD, Gordon
String trio B&H   vln, vla, vlc

CROLEY, Randell
Filament JBI   vln, vlc

EPSTEIN, David
String trio MCA   vln, vla, vlc

FRIEDELL, Harold
Elegy HWG   vln, hp, org

GABURO, Kenneth
Ideas and trans-   vla, vlc
formations nos.
2 and 3 . TP

HEIDEN, Bernhard
Inventions AB   2 vlc

OTT, Joseph
Matrix IV CBP   pno, vln, vlc

PLUMBY, Don
Picture of a hunt   vln (or fl or ob)
COL   and vlc (or bsn)

READ, Gardner
Sonoric fantasia   cel, hp, hpcd
No. 1 TP

SCHWARTZ, Elliott
3 short scenes   2 vlc
for 2 cellos AB

SCHWARTZ, Paul
Little trio MCA   pno, vln, vlc

SYDEMAN, William
Duo CFP   2 c-b

WAGNER, Joseph
Concert piece   vln, vlc
SMPC

QUARTETS
(2 vln, vla, vlc unless otherwise
indicated)

BINKERD, Gordon
String quartet No. 1 B&H
String quartet No. 2 B&H

BROWN, Earle
String quartet (1965) AMP

CHADWICK, George (H. Wiley
Hitchcock, Ed.)
String quartet in E-minor, Op. 4
(New York, 1902) DCP

CHIHARA, Paul
String quartet in one movement
SHAW

COLGRASS, Michael
Chamber music (with 4 dr) IP
(See also "Percussion")

DIAMOND, David
String quartet No. 7 SMPC
String quartet No. 10 SMPC

HARTLEY, Walter S.
String quartet No. 2 GAL

KEATS, Donald
String quartet No. 1 B&H
String quartet No. 2 B&H

KIRCHNER, Leon
String quartet No. 3 AMP

LADERMAN, Ezra
String quartet No. 1 OX
String quartet No. 3 OX

LAYTON, Billy Jim
String quartet in 2 movements GS

MASON, Daniel Gregory
Fanny Blair (folk song fantasy for
string quartet) OX

McKAY, George F.
String quartet No. 3 GAL

NEMIROFF, Isaac
    String quartet   MM(R)

SIEGMEISTER, Elie
    String quartet No. 2   MCA

SMITH, Julia
    Quartet for strings   TP

WAGNER, Joseph
    Two moments musical   RBB

WASHBURN, Robert
    String quartet   OX

WILLIS, Richard
    String quartet No. 2   TP

QUINTETS
(2 vln, vla, vlc, pno unless otherwise
    indicated)

BURTON, Eldin
    Quintet for piano and strings CF

FINNEY, Ross Lee
    Piano quintet   CFP

FOOTE, Arthur (H. Wiley
    Hitchcock, Ed.)
    Quintet for piano and strings,
        Op. 38   DCP

IVES, Charles
    The innate (with opt c-b)   PIC

POWELL, Mel
    Piano quintet   B&H

RANEY, James
    Four pieces   MJQ   5 gtr

WHITHORNE, Emerson
    Quintet, Op. 48   2 vln, 2 vla, vlc
        CF

STRINGS WITH VOICE AND/OR
WINDS, PERCUSSION

APPLEBAUM, Edward
    Montages GS   cl, vlc, pno

BARATI, George
    Octet PIC   fl, ob, hpcd,
                str quintet

BINKERD, Gordon
    Three songs for   m-S, str qrt
        mezzo-soprano and
        string quartet B&H
        (see "Solo Vocal Music")
    Trio B&H   cl, vla, vlc

CALABRO, Louis
    Five duos EV   cl, vlc

CUSTER, Arthur
    Pastorale and   vln, cl, pno
        hornpipe GEN
    Permutations GEN   vln, vlc, cl

DEL TREDICI, David
    I hear an army   S and str qrt
        B&H   text: No.
                XXXVI in
                Chamber Music
                by James Joyce

DIAMOND, David
    Elegy in memory of 4 hn, 3 trp,
        Maurice Ravel   3 trb, tba,
        (original version) perc, timp, 2 hp
        SMPC
        (See also "Per-
        cussion" and in 2nd
        edition of Catalog,
        see "String Orchestra")

DORAN, Matt
    Quartet WIM   ob, cl, bsn,
                vla
    Sonatina WIM   fl, vlc

GABURO, Kenneth
    Two   TP   m-S, fl, c-b;
                text: Virginia
                Hommel

HAUBIEL, Charles
    Pastoral trio SMC   fl, vlc, pno

IVES, Charles
    Adagio sostenuto   E-hn (or basset
        PIC   or fl), 3 vln
                (3rd vln ad lib
                or vla), vlc
                ad lib, pno or
                hp (cel or high
                bell)

KATZ, Erich
    Trio SF   2 a-rec (or
                2 fl), vla (or
                vln)

KLEIN, Lothar
Trio sonata   MJQ   cl, vlc, pno and
                    jazz set (dr)

KUBIK, Gail
Divertimento I   fl (or picc), ob
(for 13 players)   (or E-hn), b-flat
MCA(R)   cl (or b-cl), bsn,
1. Overture.   vln, vla, vlc, c-
2. Humoresque.   b, pno (or hpcd),
3. Scene change.   perc (incl. timp)
4. Seascape.
5. Burlesque.
Divertimento II   fl (or picc), ob,
(for 8 players)   cl, bsn, trp, trb,
MCA(R)   vla, pno
1. Overture and
pastorale.
2. Sound pastorale.
3. Scherzino: the
puppet show.
4. Dialogue.
5. Dance toccata.

LADERMAN, Ezra
Celestial bodies   fl, 2 vln, vla,
OX (See also   vlc
"String or
Chamber Orchestra
with Solo Instru-
ment")
Double Helix OX   fl, ob, 2 vln,
(See also   vla, vlc
"String or Cham-
ber Orchestra
with Solo
Instrument")
Nonette   OX(R)   fl, cl, bsn, trp,
                    hn, trb, vln,
                    vlc, pno
A single voice   ob, 2 vln, vla,
OX (See also   vlc
"String or Cham-
ber Orchestra
with Solo
Instrument")

LUENING, Otto
Suite for diverse   2 treble and 1
high and low   bass clef
instruments GAL

MACERO, Teo
One-three   picc (fl), vln, vlc,
quarters CFP   trb, tba, 2 pno

MALTBY, Richard
Ballad   CF   4 trp, 4 hn,
                    4 trb, tba, c-
                    b, gtr, perc

McKAY, George Frederick
Fiesta Mejicana   4 vln, 4 hn, 4
CF(R)   sax, 4 trp, 4
1. Greeting to   cl (also avail-
the sun   able for cl
2. Circle dance   quartet or sax
3. In gay mood   quartet)
4. Serenade of the
caballero
5. Con mucho gusto

MOSS, Lawrence
Remembrances for   fl, trp, vln,
8 performers   vib, cl, hn,
TP(R)   vlc, perc
1. Tranquillo.
Vivace. Tranquillo.
2. Serenata
3. Da capo.
Epilogue. (See
also "Percussion")

PLUMBY, Don
Picture of a hunt   fl (or ob or
COL   vln), bsn (or
                    vlc)

PORTER, Quincy
Quintet ("Elegiac") ob, str qrt
GAL

READ, Gardner
Sonoric fantasia   5 fl, hp, perc
No. 3 AB   (3 performers)
(See also
"Percussion")

SACCO, P. Peter
Elegie WIM   fl, vlc

SCHMIDT, William
Music for scrim-   hp, brass
shaws WIM   quintet
Of the sea and
ships. Of whales
and whaling. Of
sailors and
maidens fair.

SPIES, Claudio
Five psalms B&H   S, T, fl, bsn,
                    hn, man, vla,
                    vlc, Text:
                    Biblical

LXXXV - eights   for str and
and fives B&H   clarinets

STARER, Robert
Trio SMPC   cl, vlc, pno

STEVENS, Halsey
Three Hungarian   vla, vlc, E-hn
folk songs GAL   (or cl), pno

WEBER, Ben
Nocturne, Op. 55   fl, cel, vlc
TP

WERNICK, Richard
Stretti MIL   cl, vln, vla, gtr

WOLFF, Christian
For 5 or 10   For any group of
people   5 or 10 players
Pairs CFP   For 2, 4, 6, or
                        8 players; any
                        instruments

WOODWIND ENSEMBLES

DUOS AND TRIOS

BAKSA, Robert F.
Running tune,   fl, ob, cl
lullaby and
march SHAW

BALBO, G. C.
Three etchings   fl, cl; or ob, cl
SF

BARAB, Seymour
Little suite B&H   3 fl

BERLINSKI, Herman
Three or four-   3 (or 4) ob or 3
part canons and   (or 4) cl or 3
rounds TP   (or 4) bsn or
                        4 sax

BIALOWSKY, Marshall
Suite WIM   fl, ob, cl
March. Aria.
Fughetta.

BINKERD, Gordon
Duo B&H   fl, ob

BROWN, Newel Kay
Four pieces TP   fl, cl

BUTTS, Carrol
Moderato and   3 sax
allegro SHAW

CHILDS, Barney
Music for 2 flute   2 fl
players TP

COLF, Dorrit Licht
Three pieces for   2 fl
2 flutes MM

DAVENPORT, LaNoue
Carols for re-   3 rec (S, A, T)
corders (7 medi-
aeval carols) GAL
More carols for   3 rec (S, A, T)
recorders (7 me-
diaeval carols) GAL
Three duets SF   2 fl (or 2 ob
                        or 2 cl)

DONAHUE, Robert
Five canonic duets   fl, cl
TP

HART, William
Sonatina WIM   2 fl

HEUSSENSTAMM, George
Seven etudes WIM   ob, cl, bsn

HORVIT, Michael
Little suite SHAW   fl, cl, bsn (or
Prelude. Song.   b-cl)
Fugue. Statement.
Pleasantry.
Minuet. March.

HUGHES, Kent
Second chance   fl, ob
WIM

KATZ, Erich
Toy concerto SF   3 rec (S, A, T)
                        with keyboard
                        instr. and perc
                        (or for picc,
                        fl, cel, perc)

KELLER, Homer
Five pieces AMP   cl, bsn

KOCH, John
The recorder   Duos: S, A; S,
books of John   S; T, T: trios:
Koch GEN   S, A, T

KURTZ, S. J.
Suite   SF   3 cl
Three canonic   3 cl
  dances SF
Three impres-   2 cl
  sions SF

LEES, Benjamin
Duo   B&H   fl, cl

MAXWELL, Everett
Trio   WIM   fl, cl, bsn

MICHALSKY, Donal R.
Divertimento WIM 3 cl
Trio concertino   fl, ob, hn
  WIM

MURPHY, Lyle
Notturno WIM   3 sax

OTT, Joseph
Five pieces CBP   fl, cl

PLUMBY, Don
Picture of a   fl (or ob or vln)
  hunt   COL   and bsn (or vlc)

RAYMOND, Lewis
Divertimento WIM 3 fl

READ, Gardner
Petite suite COL   2 rec (S, A) or
                        2 fl and hpcd
                        (or pno)

ROY, Klaus George
Duo   TP   fl, cl

RUGOLO, Pete
Offbeat   WIM   fl, cl, bsn

SACCO, P. Peter
Andante and   2 fl
  cantabile WIM

STEIN, Leon
Trio   TP   3 cl (or 3 trp)

VAN VACTOR, David
Music for wood-   duos and trios
  winds Vol. 1   for various
  S-B   woodwind com-
                        binations

WALKER, Richard
Rococo KMI   ob, cl, bsn

QUARTETS
(fl, ob, cl, bsn unless otherwise
indicated)

BENAGLIA, John
Five vignettes   4 rec (S, A, T,
  GAL   B)

BENNETT, David
Clarinet rhapsody   4 cl
  CF
Prelude and   4 cl
  scherzo CF
Sax-soliloquy SMC   4 sax (also
                        available with
                        band acc)
Saxophone sym-   4 sax
  phonette CF

BOERINGER, James
Dance suite   AMP

BUTTS, Carrol
Quartet for flutes   4 fl
  SHAW

COHEN, David
Divertimento WIM   4 fl
Prelude. Chorale.
Scherzo I. Aria.
Small talk. Re'seau.
Scherzo II. Reflec-
tion. Finale.

COPPOLA, Don
Quartet for winds
  KMI

CROLEY, Randell
Tre espressioni   4 sax
  JBI

DEDRICK, Chris
Sensitivity KMI   4 sax (or ob,
                        cl, hn, bsn)

DEDRICK, Rusty
The modern art   4 sax
  suite KMI
Impressionism.
Purism. Mysti-
cism. Surrealism.
Realism.

DELAMONT, Gordon
Three entertain-   4 sax
  ments KMI

DILLON, Robert
Allegro festoso   4 cl
B&H

END, Jack
Two modern sax- 4 sax
ophone quartets
KMI
Sostentuto. Giocoso.

FINK, Robert R.
Four modes for
winds   S-B
Dorian prelude.
Lydian scherzo.
Phrygian chant.
Mixolydian març.h.

FRACKENPOHL, Arthur
Toccata   GS

FRANK, Marcel
Conversation   4 sax
piece   KMI

FULEIHAN, Anis
Humoristic pre-
ludes   SMPC
1. Overture
2. Aerobatics
3. In a barnyard
4. A serenade
   for Judy
5. Exit
(All above works
published separately)

GHENT, Emmanuel
Quartet for wood-
winds   OX

GRESHAM, Ann
Baroque lament   4 sax
JBI

KANTOR, Joseph
Serenade   WIM

LOWMAN, Kenneth
Los Angeles   4 cl
sketches   WIM
Woodland hill-
billy. Echo Park.
Olvera Street.

MAXWELL, Everett
Idylls of 4 gob-   4 bsn
lins   WIM

McCLELLAN, Randall
Three modes WIM   fl, 3 cl

McKAY, George Frederick
Episodes CLB   4 cl
Five pieces WIM   4 cl
Scene. Sailor's
dance. April.
Prarie legend.
Jubilation.
Sonatina giocosa   4 fl
CLB
Suite matinale CLB   4 fl
Suite pastorale CLB   4 fl
Three nautical
characters CLB

MURPHY, Lyle
Prelude and canon   4 sax
WIM
Rondino WIM   4 sax
Suite   WIM   4 sax

NESTICO, Sammy
A study in con-   4 sax
trasts KMI
The demure. The
delightful.

PILLIN, Boris
Scherzo WIM

ROY, Klaus George
"Sterlingman" suite TP

SPEARS, Jared
Episode SMC   4 sax
Quartet "66" SMC   4 sax

SPIES, Claudio
Canon for 4 flutes   4 fl
B&H

UBER, David
Three sketches
for 4 woodwinds
SMPC

VAN VACTOR, David
Music for wood-
winds, Vol. II
(quartets and quin-
tets for various
woodwind combi-
nations) S-B

WALKER, Richard
Suite KMI   4 sax

QUINTETS
(fl, ob, cl, bsn, hn unless otherwise
indicated)

ADLER, Samuel
Intrada   OX

BLUMENFELD, Harold
Expansions   MCA

BRITAIN, Radie
A woodwind quintet
RBB

CROLEY, Randell
Microespressioni
JBI

CUSTER, Arthur
Two movements for
woodwind quintet
GEN

DELANEY, Robert
Suite   SMC

DI DOMINICO, Robert
Quintetto   EBM

GOTTLIEB, Jack
Twilight crane (fan-
tasy for woodwind
quintet)   GS

HARTLEY, Gerald
Divertissement AMP

HELM, Everett
Woodwind quintet
AMP

HUSTON, Scott
4 conversations B&H

KINGMAN, Daniel
Quintet for winds
WIM

KOCH, Frederick
Scherzo for 5 winds
GEN

KRAFT, Leo
Partita No. 3 GEN

McKAY, George Frederick
Three nautical char-
acters   CLB

Three sea sketches
CLB
Sea birds. Chanty.
Bon voyage.

PYLE, Francis Johnson
Woodwind quintet S-C

TULL, Fisher
Suite   SHAW
Intrada. Gambol
for clarinet. Soli-
loquy for oboe.
March for horn.
Scherzo for bas-
soon. Elegy for
flute. Finale.

VAN VACTOR, David
Music for wood-
winds, Vol. II
S-B (quartets and
quintets for var-
ious woodwind
combinations)

WARD-STEINMAN, David
Montage MJQ

WASHBURN, Robert
Quintet for winds OX

ZANINELLI, Luigi
Musica drammatica (with opt
SHAW   perc)

SEXTETS, SEPTETS, OCTETS
AND LARGER ENSEMBLES

ADLER, Samuel
Seven epigrams   picc (fl 1),
OX   fl 2, ob, 2 cl,
                    bsn

BROWN, Rayner
Symphony for   cl choir
clarinets WIM

FRACKENPOHL, Arthur
Aria with fughetta 2 fl, ob, E-hn,
SHAW   7 cl, 3 bsn,
                    4 sax
Prelude and   8 cl
allegro SHAW

KLAUSS, Noah
Prelude S-B   6 cl

KLEINSINGER, George
Design for wood-   fl, ob, 2 cl,
winds   AMP   hn, bsn

KOHN, Karl
Concert music   for 12 wood-
MM   winds

LADERMAN, Ezra
Octet for winds   2 ob, 2 cl,
OX   2 hn, 2 bsn

MAURY, Lowndes
Changes for 7   7 fl
flutes WIM

NESTICO, Sammy
A study in con-   6 or 9 cl
trasts KMI

RAYMOND, Lewis
Chorale in Gre-   cl choir
gorian style WIM

VERRALL, John
Septet for winds   fl, ob, 2 cl,
GAL   hn, 2 bsn

WHITE, Donald H.
Divertissement   cl choir
COL

MIXED WOODWINDS, BRASS, VOICE,
KEYBOARD, AND/OR PERCUSSION

ARNOLD, Hubert
Sonata SMC   2 trp, pno

BASSETT, Leslie
Nonet CFP   fl, ob, cl, bsn,
                   trp, hn, trb,
                   tba, pno

BINKERD, Gordon
Studenten-   org, 2 trp, 2 hn,
Schmaus B&H   2 trb, 2 tba

BRANT, Henry
Verticals ascend-
ing after Rodia
Towers MCA(R)

Group I: 2 ob, 2 bsn,
         sax, 2 trp,
         trb, pno
Group II: picc, fl, 3 cl,
         2 hn, tba,
         perc, elec-
         tronic org
NOTE: Where strings
         are present, an
         alternate ver-
         sion is available
         (see also
         "Percussion")

CAMPO, Frank
Concentration WIM 3 cl, pno

CROLEY, Randell
Concerto for flute fl; pno/cel, 4
and metal or-   trb, tba, timp,
chestra JBI   perc
(See also
"Percussion")

de GASTYNE, Serge
Abacus in trio FER
Prelude   hn, bsn, mar
Invention   hn, bsn, vib
Burletta   hn, bsn, mar
Night music   hn, bsn, vib
Finale   hn, bsn, mar
(See also
"Percussion")

ELMORE, Robert
Concerto for   org, 3 trp, 3
brass, organ and   trb, perc
percussion HWG
(See also
"Percussion)
Fanfare for   org, trp, trb,
Easter FLAM   perc

HARTLEY, Walter S.
Double concerto   a-sax and tba
JBI   with wind octet
                   (fl, ob, cl,
                   bsn, hn, 2 trp,
                   trb)

HOVHANESS, Alan
Mountains and   fl, ob, cl, trp,
rivers without   trb, hp, timp,
end, Op. 225   perc
(Chamber sym-
phony) CFP(R)
(See also
"Percussion")

KOHN, Karl
Adagio and alle-   brass qrt, pno
  gro MM

KORTE, Karl
Matrix GAL   woodwind quin-
               tet, pno, perc

KROEGER, Karl
Toccata AB   cl, trb, perc
  (See also
  "Percussion")

MAYER, Rudolf
Sonata SMC   2 hn, pno

OWEN, Harold
Fantasies on   3 trp (cor), pno
  Mexican tunes
  WIM

POWELL, Mel
Divertimento for   fl, ob, cl, bsn,
  five winds CF   trp

PRESSER, William
Jorepi TP   cl, trb, pno

SACCO, P. Peter
Three psalms   T, brass quin-
  WIM   tet; text: Biblical

SCHMIDT, William
Chamber concerto org and brass
  WIM   quintet
Chamber music   hn, trp, trb, pno
  WIM
  Prelude. Chorale.
Concertino WIM   pno, cl choir
Concertino WIM   pno and brass
                   quintet

SCHWADRON, A. A.
Short suite KMI   cl, trb

SHORES, Richard
Mulholland suite   2 fl, cl, pno
  WIM
  Scenic drive.
  View from the
  top. Downgrade.

STARER, Robert
Concerto a tre   cl, trp, trb, pno
  MCA (Also for
  chamber orch;
  see Second Edition
  of this Catalog,
  p. 274)

TUTHILL, Burnet C.
Variations on   fl, ob, cl, hn,
  "When Johnny   bsn, pno
  comes marching
  home" GAL

UBER, David
Sonata SMPC   trp, trb, pno

VAUGHAN, Rodger
Quattro bicinie JBI cl, tba

WASHBURN, Robert
Concertino OX   fl, ob, cl, bsn,
                  2 trp, hn, trb,
                  tba

BRASS ENSEMBLES

DUOS, TRIOS AND QUARTETS

BASSETT, Leslie
Brass trio KING   hn, trp, trb

BERLINSKI, Herman
Three or four-   3 (or 4) trp
  part canons and
  rounds TP

BEYER, Frederick
Conversations JBI   hn, trp, trb

BODA, John
Prelude, scherzo,   2 trp, hn, trb
  postlude JBI

BRITAIN, Radie
Processional RBB   4 trb

BROWN, Rayner
Six fugues WIM   hn, trp, tba

CACAVAS, John
Trumpeters   3 trp
  three EBM

COLE, George
Seven impres-   3 trb, bar (Eu-
  sions AMP   phonium) or tba

DIERCKS, John
Horn quartet TP   4 hn

FRACKENPOHL, Arthur
Trio KING   hn, trp, trb

HADDAD, Don
    Two impressions   4 hn
    SHAW
    Corni da caccia.
    Alla jazz.

HARTLEY, Walter S.
    Solemn music TP   2 trp, hn, trb
    Prelude. An-   (also for brass
    them. Postlude.   choir)

HASLAM, Herbert
    Antimasque TP   2 trp, 2 trb

HAUGLAND, Archie
    Apollo AMP   4 trp

HOGG, Merle
    3 short pieces   hn, trp, trb
    JBI

HOVHANESS, Alan
    Canzona and fugue 2 trp, hn, trb
    CFP   (or tba)
    Five fantasies for
    brass CFP
        Nos. 1, 2, & 3:   hn, trp, trb
        Nos. 4 & 5:   hn, 2 trp, trb
                          (or tba)

KAUER, Gene
    Quartet WIM   4 hn

KNOX, Charles
    Solo for tuba and   tba; trp, hn, trb
    brass trio JBI

LESSARD, John
    Quodlibets GEN   2 trp, trb

LIEBERMAN, Fredric
    Leaves of brass   2 trp, hn, trb
    COL

LO PRESTI, Ronald
    Trio   SHAW   3 trb

McKAY, George Frederick
    Allegro risoluto   4 hn
        (Divertimento,
        Op. 16, No. 3)
        CF
    March (Petite   4 hn
        suite, Op. 15,
        No. 3) CF
    Nocturne (Petite   4 hn
        suite, Op. 15,
        No. 2) CF

MURPHY, Lyle
    Etude No. 1 WIM   2 trp, hn, trb

PETERSEN, Ted
    Divertimento for   trp, hn, trb
    brass trio   KMI

PRESSER, William
    Prelude, fugue and   hn, trp, trb
    postlude JBI

SCHMIDT, William
    Sonatina WIM   hn, trb, tba
    Variations WIM 4 hn

SCHOOLEY, John
    Partita KMI
        Chorale   2 trp, trb, tba
        Invention   2 trp
        Pastorale   2 trp, trb, tba
        Invention   trb, tba
        Fugato   2 trp, trb, tba
        Finale   2 trp, trb, tba

SCHRAMM, Harold
    Partita TP   2 trp

SPIES, Claudio
    Times two B&H   2 hn

STABILE, James
    Suite WIM   2 trp, 2 trb

STEIN, Leon
    Quartet UMP   2 trp, 2 trb
    Trio TP   3 trp (or 3 cl)

TANNER, Paul
    Concerto WIM   2 trb (with
                    pno acc)

TREVARTHEN, Richard
    Sonata JBI   2 trp, hn, trb

TULL, Fisher
    Canonical trilogy   4 trp
    WIM

UBER, David
    Miniature sym-   2 trp, 2trb
    phony   GS
    Suite for 4 hours   4 hn
    SMPC

WHEAR, Paul
    Prelude and rondo   2 cor, 2 trb
    CLB

QUINTETS
(2 trp, hn, trb, tba unless otherwise
indicated)

ALEXANDER, Josef
Four for five SMPC

BARON, Samuel
Impressions of a
parade (based on
"When Johnny
comes marching
home") GS

BEACH, Bennie
Music for brass
quintet TP

BROWN, Rayner
Quintet No. 2 WIM

CHILDS, Barney
Variations sur une
chanson de canotier
CF

COBINE, Albert
Trilogy KING

CROLEY, Randell
Concert music JBI

De JONG, Conrad
Essay JBI

DORSAM, Paul
Fanfare and fugato 5 trp, sn-dr
WIM (See also
"Percussion")

FARBERMAN, Harold
Five images GEN

HARTLEY, Walter S.
Divertissement CF

HOGG, Merle
Invention JBI

HOVHANESS, Alan
Six dances CFP

HUGGLER, John
Quintet KING

JONES, Charles
4 movements for
5 brass KING

KORN, Peter Jona
Prelude and scherzo
B&H

KORTE, Karl
Introductions for
brass quintet EV

KROEGER, Karl
Partita TP

OTT, Joseph
Toccata CBP

PERSICHETTI, Vincent
Parable II EV

PINKHAM, Daniel
Prelude, adagio   unison ch ad
and chorale CFP   lib; text: Bibli-
                    cal (Psalm 134)

PRESSER, William
Brass quintet
(1965) JBI

RIDDLE, Nelson
Three-quarter suite
MCA

ROSENTHAL, Irving
Three Renaissance
madrigals WIM
  I. Jubilate Deo
     (after Gregor
     Aichinger)
  II. Dolorasi Mar-
     tin, fieri
     tormenti (after
     Luzzasco
     Luzzagchi)
  III. Revency venir
     du printans
     (after Claude
     Le Jeune)

SCHMIDT, William
Seven variations on a
hexachord WIM
Suite No. 2 (folk-
songs) WIM
"Rosetree".
"Plaintive song"
(original). "Coal
vendor's call".

SIEGMEISTER, Elie
  Sextet for brass   brass quintet
  and percussion   and perc
  MCA (See also
  "Percussion")

SPEARS, Jared
  Four miniatures TP
  Prelude. Burlesque.
  Nocturne. March.

TULL, Fisher
  Exhibition (demon-
  stration piece) WIM

WAGNER, Joseph
  Three charades SMPC
  Buffoons. Phan-
  toms. Gossips.

WEILLE, F. Blair
  Suite for brass
  quintet   TP
  Jazz fanfare.
  Slow movement.
  Scherzo. March.

SEXTETS

DIETZ, Norman C.
  Modern moods   2 trp, hn, trb,
  AMP   bar, tba

GLASS, Philip
  Suite for brass   2 trp, 2 trb,
  sextet HWG   hn, tba

McKAY, George
  Frederick
  Legends CLB   2 trp, hn, trb,
                      bar, tba
  Prelude and   2 trp, hn, trb,
  allegro CLB   bar, tba
  Moods in con-   2 trp, hn, trb,
  trast CLB   bar, tba
  Pastoral poem.
  Fantastic scherzo.

OTT, Joseph
  Suite for six tubas 6 tba
  CBP

SCHMIDT, William
  Sequential fanfares 6 trp, perc
  WIM (See also
  "Percussion")

TANNER, Paul
  El cangrejo (the   6 trb, perc
  crab) WIM
  (See also
  "Percussion")

LARGE BRASS ENSEMBLES

ADLER, Samuel
  Five vignettes   12-part trb
  OX(R)   choir

BARBER, Samuel
  Mutations from   3 trp, 4 hn, 3
  Bach   GS   trb, tba, timp
  (Transforma-
  tions of the plain-
  song: "Christe,
  du lamm Gottes")

BINKERD, Gordon
  Three canzonas   3 trp, 3 hn,
  B&H   3 trb, tba

DVORAK, Robert
  Lament and repose   2 trp, 2 hn,
  COL   bar, 3 trb, tba

FLAGELLO, Nicolas
  Concertino GEN   4 hn, 2 trp, 3
                      trb, tba, timp,
                      pno

HADDAD, Don
  Fugue in D-minor   3 trp, 3 hn, 3
  SHAW   trb, tba, sock
                      cmb

HOVHANESS, Alan
  Requiem and re-   2 trp, 4 hn, 3
  surrection CFP   trb, tba, timp,
  (See also   perc
  "Percussion")

KRAFT, William
  Nonet for brass   2 trp, hn, trb,
  and percussion   tba, perc, qrt
  WIM (See also
  "Percussion")

LEBOW, Leonard
  Suite for brass   3 trp, 3 hn, 3
  S-B   trb, bar-trb,
  March. Blues.   tba, perc, timp
  Reel. (See also   (or for brass
  "Percussion")   octet: 3 trp, hn,
                      3 trb, tba)

MALTBY, Richard
Ballad for brass 4 trp, 4 hn, 4
choir and per- trb, tba, c-b,
cussion CF gtr, perc
(See also
"Percussion")

MERRIMAN, Thomas
Theme and 4 4 trp, 2 hn, 3
variations AMP trb, bar, tba

OTT, Joseph
Suite for 8 8 trb
trombones CBP

SACCO, P. Peter
Introduction and 3 trp, 4 hn, 3
lament WIM trb, tba
Study for brass 3 trp, 2 trb,
and percussion bar, tba, timp,
(See also perc
"Percussion") WIM

SCHMIDT, William
Chorale, march 3 trp, 4 hn, 3
and fugato WIM trb, bar, tba,
(See also timp, perc
"Percussion")
Fanfare 1969 WIM 8 trp
Four songs for 3 trp, 4 hn, 3
brass and per- trb, bar, tba,
cussion WIM timp, perc, hp
(See also (opt)
"Percussion")
Trois chansons 4 trp, 4 hn, 4
de Vincennes trb, bar, tba,
WIM (See also timp, perc
"Percussion")

STARER, Robert
Serenade for for combination
brass SMPC of 11 brass instr

THOMSON, Virgil
Ode to the won- 3 trp, 2 hn, 3
ders of nature trb, timp, sn-
GS (See also dr, field dr
"Percussion")

TULL, Fisher
Liturgical sym- 6 trp, 4 hn, 4
phony WIM trb, 2 bar, 2
(See also tba, timp, perc
"Percussion")
Variations on an 6 trp, 4 hn, 4
Advent theme trb, 2 bar, 2
WIM (See also tba, timp, perc
"Percussion")

UBER, David
Evolution I for brass choir
SMPC (instr not
available)

The power and for brass choir
the glory SMPC (instr not
Prelude. Hymn. available)
Ritual dance.
Spiritual.

ZANINELLI, Luigi
Jubilate Deo for brass choir
SHAW (instr not
available)

4. CONCERT JAZZ

JAZZ COMBOS AND BIG BAND CONCERT JAZZ

CHRISTIAN, Bobby
and Coles A. Doty
Blue fog TP	solo trp, 4 trp, 5 sax, 4 trb, hn, pno, c-b, vib, dr, gtr
Linda's lament TP	same instr as above
Now it's spring TP	same instr as above
River's end TP	same instr as above
To whom may we turn TP	same instr as above

CURNOW, Robert
Festival piece KSM	5 sax, 5 trp, hn, 4 trb, tba, rhythm section (gtr, c-b, dr, pno) Separate parts are available for fl and cl if saxes do not double.

KRAFT, William
Configurations (a
concerto for 4
percussion soloists
and jazz orchestra
MCA(R) (See also
"Percussion")

MORGAN, Robert
Anadge KSM	5 sax, 5 trp, 5 trb
T-bones KSM	5 sax, 5 trp, 5 trb, gtr, pno, c-b, dr

5. PERCUSSION

BACH, Jan
  Turkish music CPC

sn-dr, t-dr, b-dr, tam, susp cmb

BALES, Richard
  American design
  (National Gallery suite No. 3)
  AB(R)
  (For contents, see "Small or
  Chamber Orchestra")

cham orch and perc: side dr, sn-dr, b-dr, cmb, susp cmb, gong (deep), tam, tom-tom, wood block, glock, xy, tri, hooves, rattle, slide whistle

BAUERNSCHMIDT, Robert
  Mezozoic fantasy MP

xy, chimes, wood block, 2 temple blocks, tri, cmb, gong, claves, tom-tom, sn-dr I, sn-dr II, 3 timp, b-dr

BELLSON, Louis
  Four stories WIM

4 complete dr sets

BENCRISCUTTO, Frank
  Rondeau for percussion (8
  players) MP

instr not available

BENSON, Warren
  Three dances for solo snare drum
  CHAP
  Cretan dance. Fox trot. Fandango.

sn-dr

BRANT, Henry
  Verticals ascending after Rodia
  Towers MCA

Group II: picc, fl, 3 cl, 2 hn, tba, electronic org, perc: 2 players - timp, chimes, glock, vib

BROWN, Earle
  Hodograph I AMP

orch bells, vib, mar, fl, pno, cel

BROWN, Thomas
  Ensembolero KMI

Perc I: sn-dr, b-dr, cmb; Perc II: bongos; Perc III: 2 tom-tom; Perc IV: timp, pno

  Pattern percussion KMI
  (See also "Band")
  Percussionata KMI
  (See also "Band")

tom-tom, sn-dr, bongos, b-dr, timp

perc ensemble with band acc

BROWNE, Donald
  Three by three LMP

2 timp, tri, b-dr, sn-dr

BUGGERT, Robert W.
  Dialogue for solo percussion and
  piano CPC

sn-dr, field dr, tom-tom, pno

Fanfare, song and march CPC sn-dr, wood block, tri, tom-tom, tam-tam, susp cmb, bells, pno

J-21557 CPC sn-dr solo

Short overture for percussion CPC sn-dr, tam, tri, bongos, 2 timp

Toccata No. 1 CPC sn-dr, wood block, tri, tam, claves, bongos, susp cmb, b-dr

BURGE, David
Sources III AB cl and perc: lujon (8 tones), cmb, tri, vib, 3 wood blocks, tom-tom, 2 congo dr, b-dr, large tam-tam

CARTER, Elliott
8 pieces for 4 timpani (one 4 timp
  player) AMP
  1. Saëta. 2. Moto perpetuo.
  3. Adagio. 4. Recitative.
  5. Improvisation. 6. Canto.
  7. Canaries. 8. March.
  (The composer specifies that not
  more than 4 of the pieces are
  ever to be played as a suite in
  public, with movements 4, 5,
  7, 8 as outer ones; the others
  as inner.)

CEROLI, Nick
Triple threat WIM 2 sn-dr, t-dr

CLARK, Owen
Quasi bossa nova LMP 5 players: perc ensemble or dr corps of 2 sn-dr, t-dr, b-dr, cow bell

COLEMAN, Gary
Percussion quintet WIM chimes, vibes, tri, sn-dr, susp cmb, timp

COLGRASS, Michael
Chamber music IP 4 dr and str quintet
Divertimento IP 8 dr, pno, str orch
Inventions on a motive (motive, 1. 4 high dr turntable, small cow-
  6 inventions and finale) MP bell, 2 wood blocks. 2. 2 bongos, tri, 3 cowbells, cmb. 3. timbales, 2 cmb, cowbells. 4. 3 timp.

COMBS, F. Michael
Gesture for solo percussionist CPC sn-dr, tom-tom, b-dr, susp cmb

CROLEY, Randell
Concerto for flute and metal solo fl, pno/cel, 4 trb, tba, timp,
  orchestra JBI perc I, II, III

de GASTYNE, Serge
Abacus in trio FER
  Prelude hn, bsn, mar
  Invention hn, bsn, vib
  Burletta hn, bsn, mar

Night music   hn, bsn, vib
Finale   hn, bsn, mar
Ballata for vibraharp solo   FER
Perpetual motion for vibes solo FER
Preludes 1 - 8 for vibes solo   FER
Quintet for mallet percussion FER
Toccata for marimba solo   FER

DIAMOND, David
Elegy in memory of Maurice   4 hn, 3 trp, 3 trb, tba, 2 hp, timp,
Ravel (original version)   SMPC   perc (1 player): t-dr, glock, deep
                                               gong

DORSAM, Paul
Fanfare and fugato   WIM   5 trp, sn-dr

DUCKWORTH, William
The journey   CPC   solo perc

ELMORE, Robert
Concerto for brass, organ and   org, 3 trp, 3 trb, perc: sn-dr,
percussion   HWG   bells, cmb, tri, timp

FARAGO, Marcel
Rhythm and colors, Op. 19A CPC   4 timp, 4 tom-toms, xy, 2 tri, cmb,
                                               gong, vib, 2 pairs finger cmb, bells,
                                               chimes, wood block, tam, b-dr,
                                               temple block, castanets

FELDSTEIN, Saul
Timetable   AMC   dr set solo
(See also "Band")

FETLER, Paul
A contemporary psalm   AUG   SATB ch with S and Bar solos, org,
                                               perc: timp, 2 dr, cmb, gong, finger
                                               cmb, wood block, cel, chimes,
                                               glock; text by Chester A. Pennington

FOSS, Lukas
Paradigm   CF(R)   Percussionist-conductor (one man).
(NOTE: Of the four movements   Perc instruments are: musical saw,
in this work, three make use of   flexation, vib, cmb, gong, sn-dr,
words which are to be said,   susp antique cmb, tam, 5 blocks,
whispered or shouted. To quote   superball. In addition, the score
the composer, "Words are   calls for an electric guitar or elec-
handled like notes." The move-   tric sitar and three other instruments are I Session, II Reading,   ments capable of sustaining a sound
III Recital, IV Lecture. The   (if string instruments are used, con-
choice of English, French or   tact mikes will be needed for move-
German text is made available   ments I and IV.)
for movements I and II. Move-   Text by composer.
ment III is purely instrumental.
For movement IV, one is to
choose either the English text or
the mixture of all three languages
that appears under the English text.
Movement IV also makes use of
tape to imitate the live performance.)

FRACKENPOHL, Arthur
Hogamus, higamus (double fugue
for speaking chorus and percussion) EBM

SAB or SSA or TBB ch with perc:
(1 or 3 players)
metals - blocks, tri or cmb
woods - wood or temple blocks
membranes - timbales, bongos, tom-
toms, congas or dr;
Text: anon

FROCK, George and John Warrington
Drums of America   TP
(See also "Band")

band and perc: field dr, xy, sn-dr,
tom-tom, bells, cmb, mar, glock,
b-dr, timp

FROCK, George
Concertino for marimba and
piano   SMC
Variations   SMC

fl and perc: 4 tom-toms of graduated
pitch, b-dr, susp cmb, wood block,
tri, vib

GOODMAN, Saul
Timpiana   MIL

timp, dr, cmb

GOULD, Morton
Parade   CHAP

Perc I: 2 sn-dr; Perc II: marching
machine, cmb; Perc III: 2 b-dr

GUTCHE, Gene
Bongo divertimento GAL
(See also "String or Chamber
Orchestra with Solo")

solo bongos with cham orch

HALL, Rex
Percussive panorama   LMP

xy, mar, sn-dr, bells, tri, castanets, tam, chimes, slap stick, wood
blocks, b-dr, temple blocks, mara-
cas, cmb, claves, bongos, timp

HARRISON, Lou
Suite (5 players)   MP

instr not available

HEIM, Alyn
Fanfare for percussion   MP

1. sn-dr; 2. tom-tom; 3. cmb;
4. b-dr, tam; 5. timp

HOVHANESS, Alan
Bacchanale   CFP
Mountains and rivers without
end, Op. 225 (Chamber sym-
phony)   CFP(R)
Requiem and resurrection   CFP

glock, 2 vib, chimes, giant tam-tam
fl, ob, cl, trp, trb, hp, perc I:
glock, tam-tam; perc II: vib;
perc III: chimes
2 trp, 4 hn, 3 trb, tba, perc: timp,
sn-dr, b-dr, tam-tam

JEMISON, Danys
Quintession (etude for percussion
ensemble) WIM

sn-dr, bongo dr, cmb, field dr,
b-dr

KOHS, Ellis B.
Sonata for snare drum and
piano   CPC

sn-dr, pno

KRAFT, William
Configurations (a concerto for
4 percussion soloists and
jazz orchestra) MCA(R)
(See also "Jazz Combos and
Big Band Jazz")

Perc I: 4 timp, mar, xy, tam-tam,
crotales; Perc II: crotales, bells,
chimes, b-dr, wood dr; Perc III: b-
dr, vib, 6 graduated membranic dr;
Perc IV: chimes, b-dr, crotales

French suite WIM

perc solo

Nonet for brass and percussion
WIM

2 trp, hn, trb, tba, perc: Perc I:
xy, glock, susp cmb, tri beaters;
Perc II: 4 graduated dr, vib, large
tam-tam, chimes, cmb; Perc III:
gongs, large tam-tam, chimes,
large b-dr, sizzle cmb, vib; Perc
IV: 5 timp, susp cmb, tri, gongs,
large tam-tam, cmb or temple bell

Scherzo a dué WIM

Perc I: sn-dr and field dr; Perc II:
b-dr

Trio for percussion MCA

instr not available

2-4-1 WIM

perc solo for sn-dr or any 2 perc
instr

KRAUSE, Kenneth C.
Little suite (5 players) MP

instr not available

KROEGER, Karl
Toccata AB

cl, trb, perc: vib, timp, mar, gong,
4 temple blocks, 2 susp cmb, tri

LACKEY, Douglas
Drum and coca WIM

perc sextet: 2 sn-dr, 2 t-dr, cmb,
b-dr

LATIMER, James F.
Motif for percussion CPC

sn-dr, wood block, 4 tuned dr (or 4
tom-toms), tri, susp cmb, temple
blocks, 4 timp

LEBOW, Leonard
Suite for brass S-B
March. Blues. Reel.

3 trp, 3 hn, 3 trb, bar-trb, tba,
perc, timp

LEFEVER, Maxine
De Chelly (percussion quintet) KMI
Desert KMI
Dolores KMI
Durango KMI

3 sn-dr, b-dr, cmb
2 sn-dr
sn-dr solo
2 sn-dr, cmb, b-dr

LEWIS, Robert Hall
Toccata AB

solo vln and perc (2 players): sn-dr,
t-dr, wood block, susp cmb, xy,
glock, timp

LUBOFF, Norman
African mass WMC
(For contents, see "Mixed Chorus")

SATB ch and tuned dr; text: liturgical

MALTBY, Richard
   Ballad for brass choir and per-   4 trp, 4 hn, 4 trb, tba, c-b, gtr,
     cussion   CF   perc

MARVIN, Harry
   Variety   MP   sn-dr

McAFEE, Don
   A choric psalm   CF   SATB speaking ch, perc (3 players):
                              tam, cmb, dr; text: Biblical

McDONNEL, A. E.
   Invasion   LMP   2 sn-dr, bells, t-dr, gong, tam,
                              b-dr, cmb, wood blocks, claves,
                              maracas

MOORE, James L.
   Characters three (4 players) LMP   sn-dr, tam, castanets, timp, cmb,
     1. Bolero   wood block, b-dr
     2. Swinging
     3. Latin-like
   Latisha   LMP   sn-dr solo
   Soliloquy and scherzo   LMP   fl, cel, perc: mar, cmb, tri, bells,
                              tom-toms, b-dr, blocks
   Sonata No. 1   LMP   t-dr, 2 sn-dr, vib, susp cmb, temple
                              blocks, 3 b-dr, 2 bongos, wood block

MOREY, Charles
   Bunker and San Juan hills   KMI   sn-dr duet
   A real drag   KMI   sn-dr solo

MOSS, Lawrence
   Remembrances for eight per-   fl, trp, vln, cl, hn, vlc, perc: vib,
     formers   TP(R)   t-dr, sn-dr, susp cmb, bongos,
     (For contents, see "Strings with   tubular bells, tam-tam
     Voice and/or Winds, Percussion")

MUCZYNSKI, Robert
   Statements for percussion (for   tri, cmb, tam-tam, tam, sn-dr,
     4 or 5 players)   GS   wood block, 3 timp, b-dr

NOAK, F.
   Fantasy scherzo   MP   timp

OTT, Joseph
   Quartet for percussion (for 4   timp, mallet perc, general perc 1
     players)   CBP   and 2
   Ricercare for percussion (for 3   timp, pno, general perc
     players)   CBP
   Ricercare No. 2 for percussion   timp, pno, mallet perc, general
     (for 5 players)   CBP   perc 1 and 2
   Two etudes for solo timpani CBP   4 dr

PEARSON, Robert
   Concert piece for winds and per-   instr not available
     cussion   SHAW
     (See also "Band")

PERRY, C. F.
  Homunculus (for 10 players) SMPC   4 timp, 2 susp cmb, plate cmb,
                                       sn-dr, b-dr, 2 wood blocks, xy,
                                       vib, pno, hp, cel

PETERS, G. David
  Neumes treibend   CPC   sn-dr, tom-tom, susp cmb, 2 timp

PETERS, Mitchell
  A la samba (for 6 players) KSM   instr not available
  Introductions and waltz KSM   4 tom-toms, susp cmb
  Piece for percussion (for 4   instr not available
    players) KSM
  Rondo KSM   4 tom-toms
  Sonata allegro KSM   mar, pno

PYLE, Francis Johnson
  Sonata for three   LPI   cl, pno, perc: 4 timp, 1 small and
                                       1 large tom-tom, susp cmb, xy,
                                       sn-dr

RAMEY, Phillip
  Capriccio   CPC   4 timp, crash cmb, susp cmb, tri,
                                       gong, wood block, sn-dr, b-dr

RAPHLING, Sam
  Suite for piano and percussion BI   pno, perc ensemble (instr not
                                       available)
  Timpani concerto   MP   5 dr

RAPP, John J.
  Skirmish for percussion quintet   1. sn-dr; 2. sn-dr; 3. 2 pedal timp;
    WIM   4. b-dr; 5. 3 tom-toms (pno, opt,
                                       which may be added if player 1 or 3
                                       does not play pno)

RAUSCHENBERG, Dale
  Discussion   WIM   3 sn-dr, 3 tom-toms, timp
  What?   WIM   sn-dr, bongos, tri, cmb, timp,
                                       tam, tambour, cowbell, quiro

READ, Gardner
  Los Dioses Aztecas (The Aztec   4 sn-dr, 4 tom-toms, 2 t-dr, 2 b-
    gods: suite for percussion   dr, 3 tam, 3 wood blocks, 7 susp
    ensemble)   CPC   cmb, sizzle cmb, 4 gongs, 5 antique
    1. Xiuhtecuhtli: Dios del fuego   cmb, thunder sheet, chimes, sand-
    (God of fire)   paper blocks, 3 tri, mar, vibra-
    2. Mictecacihuatl: Diosa de los   harp, chimes, glock, xy, temple
    Muertos (Goddess of the dead)   blocks, 4 timp, 2 raspers, 2 pair
    3. Tlaloc: Dios de la lluvia   claves, maracas, 1 pair cmb
    (God of rain)
    4. Tezcatlipoca: Dios de la noche
    (God of night)
    5. Xochipilli: Dios de la alegria
    y la danza   (God of pleasure
    and dance)
    6. Coyolxauhqui: Diosa de la luna
    (Goddess of the moon)

7. Huitzilopochtli: Dios de la
guerra (God of war)
Sonoric fantasia No. 3 AB   5 fl, hp, perc (3 players) (instr
                                         not available)

ROSS, Walter
Five dream sequences B&H   perc qrt and pno

RUSSELL, Armand
Two archaic dances BI   vib or mar, pno

SACCO, P. Peter
Study for brass and percussion WIM 3 trp, 2 trb, bar, tba, timp, perc

SCHMIDT, William
Chorale, march and fugato WIM   3 trp, 4 hn, 3 trb, bar, tba, timp,
                                         perc
Four songs for brass and percus-   3 trp, 4 hn, 3 trb, bar, tba, timp,
   sion WIM   perc, hp (opt)
Septigrams WIM   fl, pno, perc (1 player)
Sequential fanfares WIM   6 trp, perc
Trois chansons de Vincennes WIM   4 trp, 4 hn, 4 trb, bar, tba, timp,
                                         perc

SCHRAMM, Harold
Alarippu   MCA   SATB speaking ch and perc (instr
                                         not available); text: arranged from
                                         Bharata Natyam by Harold Schramm

SCHWARTZ, Elliott
Magic music for orchestra,   perc: 2 players (instr not available);
   piano and other sounds AB(R)   auxiliary sounds: 2 electronic re-
   (See also "Full Symphony with   production systems, i.e., phono-
   Solo")   graphs, radios, tape recorders, or 2
                                         of any combination of these. 2
                                         players needed for each system.

SEAWELL, Brent
Scope: tympany concerto No. 1   1. 5 timp dr; 2. susp cmb, gong;
   WIM   3. finger cmb, b-dr; 4. sn-dr,
                                         tom-tom

SIEGMEISTER, Elie
Sextet for brass and percussion   2 trp, hn, trb, tba, perc (1 or 2
   MCA   players): 3 pedal timp, sn-dr, 2
                                         bongos, 2 timbales, 2 tom-toms, 3
                                         temple blocks, cmb, xy, vib

TAGAWA, Rickey
Inspirations diabolique WIM   perc solo: susp cmb, bongos, tam,
   1. Introduction   sn-dr, field dr, b-dr
   2. Dance
   3. Adagio - tarantella
   4. Cadenza
   5. Perpetual motion

TANNER, Paul
El cangrejo (the crab) WIM   6 tom-toms, cmb, sn-dr, b-dr,
                                     block, maracas

THOMSON, Virgil
Ode to the wonders of nature GS   3 trp, 2 hn, 3 trb, timp, sn-dr,
                                     field dr

TULL, Fisher
Liturgical symphony   WIM   6 trp, 4 hn, 4 trb, 2 bar, 2 tba,
                                     timp, perc
Variations on an Advent theme   6 trp, 4 hn, 4 trb, 2 bar, 2 tba,
  WIM   timp, perc

VORE, Val S.
Judgement (for 6 players) LMP   sn-dr, field dr, bells, cmb, gong,
                                     chimes, timp

WILLIAMS, Clifton
Concertino for percussion and   sn-dr, t-dr, b-dr, cmb
  band   S-B
  (See also "Band")

WILLIAMS, Jan
Variations for solo kettledrums   kettledrums
  MP

WILLIAMS, Kent J.
African sketches (for 4 players)   players use African instr or sub-
  LMP   stitutes

6. ORCHESTRA

STRING ORCHESTRA	Duration* (min)		Duration* (min)
AITKEN, Hugh		JOHNSTON, Jack	
Short suite OX	5	Pastorale and fugue EV	NA
Overture. Song. Noc-			
turne. March. Finale		KIRK, Theron	
		Hemis dance CF(R)	NA
DIEMER, Emma Lou			
Pavane CF	3	KORTE, Karl	
		Song and dance (for double	8
FOOTE, Arthur (H. Wiley		string orchestra) GAL	
Hitchcock, Ed.)			
Serenade and suites in		LANE, Richard	
D-major and E-major		String song CF	2
for strings DCP	NA**		
		OTT, Joseph	
GORDON, Philip		Elegy CBP	4
Exotic dance EV	2		
		REED, Alfred	
GOULD, Morton		Titania's nocturne EBM	4
Spirituals for strings	16		
CHAP		SCHRAMM, Harold	
6 settings for double		Mogul set B&H	4
string choir and harp			
		WASHBURN, Robert	
GRAVES, William		Sinfonietta OX	11
Passacaglia and fugue MIL	6		
		WEINER, Lawrence	
HARTLEY, Walter S.		Elegy SMC	6
Psalm for strings TP	5		
HUSTON, Scott			
Two images GEN	7		

SMALL OR CHAMBER ORCHESTRA

		Duration* (min)
BALES, Richard		17
American design	fl (picc), ob (E-hn), 2 cl,	
(National Gallery Suite No. 3)	bsn, 2 hn, 2 trp, trb, 5	
AB(R)	timp, perc (2 players), str	

*Approximate

**In a few instances, the timings in minutes for the orchestral works
were not indicated in the scores or from information received from
the publishers. In those cases, the symbol "NA" is used.

1. Sign from the Black Horse Inn,   Duration
Saybrook, Connecticut.   (min)
Music: "There is a tavern in the
town"
2. Figurehead, "Jenny Lind, "
from the ship, "Nightingale"
Music: "Shenandoah"
3. Rag doll
Music: "Little Liza Jane"
4. Angel Gabriel Weathervane
Music: "The shepherds' carol"
5. Cigar store Indian
Music: "Bonny Eloise, belle of
the Mohawk Vale"
6. Whiskey flask
Music: "Old Rosin the bow" and
"Rye whiskey"
7. Dowry or "Hope" chest
Music: "Long, long ago"
8. Baseball player
Music: "Union ball club" march
          "Tally one for me"
          "Baseball" polka
(See also "Percussion")

BERGSMA, William
Dances from a New England   instr not available   8
   album, 1856   GAL
   1. Cotillion
   2. Song
   3. Waltz
   4. Quadrille

CAZDEN, Norman
Six definitions for instrumental   fl, ob, E-hn, 3 sax,   6
   ensemble   AMP   c-bsn, 2 hn, trp, pno, str

COPLAND, Aaron
Prelude from First Symphony   instr not available   5
   (arr. by composer) B&H

DIAMOND, David
Concerto for small orchestra   instr not available   NA
   SMPC(R)

IVES, Charles
Fugue from Symphony No. 4   fl, cl, hn (or trb),   8
   AMP   org (opt), timp, str

LADERMAN, Ezra
Stanzas   OX(R)   2 fl, ob, 2 cl, bsn, hn,   21
                                   trp, trb, tba, timp,
                                   perc, org, str

LAZAROF, Henri
Omaggio, a chamber concerto   instr not available   NA
   AMP(R)

Duration*
(min)

ROREM, Ned			
Water music	B&H(R)	fl (doubling picc), ob (doubling E-hn), bsn, hn, perc, hp, pno (doubling cel), str	17
SCHICKELE, Peter			
The civilian barber (overture) EV		instr not available	3
THOMSON, Virgil			
Tango lullaby (portrait of mademoiselle Alvarez de Toledo) GS		fl (picc), E-hn, cl, bsn, bells, str	4

STRING OR CHAMBER ORCHESTRA WITH SOLO INSTRUMENT OR VOICE

	Solo	Duration* (min)
ARGENTO, Dominick		
Divertimento B&H(R)	pno; str	17
BARAB, Seymour		
Tales of rhyme and reason B&H(R) Always arguing. Braggarty rabbit. A kiss from Alice. "The lordly lion." What will the neighbors say?	Narr and dance pantomime; cham; texts: Seymour Barab and Aesop fables	15
CAGE, John		
Concerto CFP(R)	prepared pno; cham	19.5
COLGRASS, Michael		
Divertimento IP (See also "Percussion")	8 dr, pno; str	6
DEL TREDICI, David		
Syzygy B&H(R)	S; woodwind octet, hn, 2 trp, tabular bells, str sextet; text: from "Ecce Puer" and "Nightpiece" by James Joyce	5
DIAMOND, David		
Concertino SMPC(R)	pno; cham	12
FULEIHAN, Anis		
Concertino B&H(R)	bsn; cham	9
Epithalamium GS(R)	pno; str	14
Suite concertante B&H(R)	fl; str	15
GOULD, Elizabeth		
Andante EV(R)	trp; str	5

*Approximate

	Solo	Duration (min)
GUTCHE, Gene Bongo divertimento GAL(R) (See also "Percussion")	bongos; cham	NA
HOVHANESS, Alan Haroutiun (resurrection) CFP(R) Aria and fugue	trp; str	10
KOHN, Karl Concerto mutabile CF(R)	pno; str or cham or str qrt	13
LADERMAN, Ezra Celestial bodies OX(R) Concerto OX(R) Double Helix OX(R) A single voice OX(R)	fl; str vln; cham fl, ob; cham ob; cham	7 26.5 15 10
LESSON, Cecil Concertino SMC Dialogue. Song and recitation. In a fairly fast four.	sax; cham or wind symphonette	NA
NEMIROFF, Isaac Concertino MM(R)	fl, vln, ob; str	NA
READ, Gardner Sonoric fantasia No. 2 (1965) TP(R)	vln; cham	12.5
SHAUGHNESSY, Robert Concertino SMPC(R)	tba; str	NA
SIEGMEISTER, Elie Dick Whittington and his cat (a symphonic story for children) MCA(R)	Narr (either an actor or [Baritone] singer) text: Edward Mabley	19
THOMSON, Virgil Autumn (concertino) GS(R)	hp; str, perc	8
TRIMBLE, Lester Duo concertante CFP(R)	2 vln; cham (also available for full symphony acc)	18
VINCENT, John Consort MIL(R)	pno; str (also with str qrt)	20
WEINER, Stanley Concerto MCA(R)	hn; str	15

FULL SYMPHONY ORCHESTRA
for classical orchestra (winds in pairs) or larger

	Duration* (min)		Duration (min)
ALLANBROOK, Douglas Four orchestral land- scapes B&H(R) Fall. Winter. Spring. Summer.	NA	COPLAND, Aaron Canticle of freedom B&H(R)	10
		CORIGLIANO, John Elegy GS(R)	7.5
AVSHALOMOV, Jacob Phases of the great land GAL(R)	16	COWELL, Henry Carol for orchestra (composer's own version	9
BARBER, Samuel Symphony No. 1, Op. 9 GS(R)	18.5	for "Western" orchestra of 2nd movement of his Koto Concerto) AMP(R)	
BASSETT, Leslie Colloquy CFP(R)	10	CRESTON, Paul Airborne suite SHAW(R)	
BEESON, Jack Symphony No. 1 in A- major MCA(R) Transformations MCA(R)	20 10	Afternoon in Montreal Night in Mexico (NOTE: The other 2 movements of the suite, "Evening in Texas" and	4 4
BERGSMA, William Documentary one: Por- trait of a city GAL(R)	17	"Sunrise in Puerto Rico" are available on rental basis) Chthonic ode GS(R)	NA
BINKERD, Gordon Movement for orchestra B&H(R)	11	DAY, Richard Grief SHAW	5
Symphony No. 1 B&H(R) Symphony No. 2 B&H(R) Symphony No. 3 B&H(R) Sun singer B&H(R)	23 27 12 10	DELLO JOIO, Norman Five images for orchestra EBM Homage to Haydn EBM(R)	6 14
CARTER, Elliott Concerto for orchestra AMP(R)	23	DIAMOND, David Overture to "The Tem- pest" CHAP(R) Symphony No. 1 SMPC(R) Symphony No. 3 SMPC(R) Symphony No. 5 SMPC(R)	4 20 26 17
CHADWICK, George W. (H. Wiley Hitchcock, Ed.) Symphony No. 2 (1886) DCP	16		
COLGRASS, Michael As quiet as MCA(R) A leaf turning colors. An uninhabited creek. An ant walking. Children sleeping. Time passing. A soft rainfall. The first star coming out.	23	DIEMER, Emma Lou Festival overture EV FOSS, Lukas Baroque variations CF(R) 1. on a Handel larghetto 2. on a Scarlatti sonata 3. on a Bach prelude (Phorion)	4 25

*Approximate

	Duration (min)
FOSTER, Stephen (H. Wiley Hitchcock, Ed.) The social orchestra (New York, 1854 - a collection of arrangements by Foster of many of his own songs, including the sets of quadrilles) DCP	varies
FREED, Arnold Alleluia for orchestra B&H(R)	9
GORDON, Philip Northern saga COL	3
GOULD, Morton Dance variations CHAP(R) Family album CHAP(R) Minstrel show CHAP(R) Philharmonic waltzes CHAP(R)	23 15 7.5 9
GRUNDMAN, Clare American folk rhapsody B&H Two sketches B&H	6.5 3.5
GUTCHE, Gene Hsiang Fei, Op. 40 GAL(R)	15
HARRIS, Roy Symphony No. 5 MIL(R)	23
HORVIT, Michael Toccatina SHAW	2.5
IMBRIE, Andrew Legend SHAW(R)	14
JAMES, Philip Brennan on the moor SMPC(R)	8
JOHNSON, Hunter Past the evening sun GAL(R)	8.5
KOHN, Karl Three scenes for orchestra CF(R)	11.5
LAZAROF, Henri Mutazione (1967) AMP(R)	13
LEES, Benjamin Symphony No. 3 B&H(R)	20

	Duration (min)
LUENING, Otto Kentucky rondo GAL(R)	6
MITCHELL, Lyndol "Ballad" from Kentucky Mountain Portraits CF "Cindy" from Kentucky Mountain Portraits CF	4 4
PAINE, John Knowles (H. Wiley Hitchcock, Ed.) Symphony No. 1 (1876) DCP Symphony No. 2 ("Im Frūling") (1880) DCP	NA NA
PETERSON, Wayne Exaltation, dithyramb and caprice B&H(R) Free variations for orchestra B&H(R)	27 20
PISTON, Walter Ricercare AMP(R)	11
PRESSER, William Arctic night EV	6
REED, Alfred A festival prelude EBM	5
SCHUMAN, William Evocation - to thee old cause TP(R) In praise of Shahn (canticle for orchestra) TP(R) Symphony No. 9 ("Le Fosse Ardeatine") TP(R)	17 17.5 28
SIEGMEISTER, Elie Five fantasies of the theater MCA(R) Beckett. Ionesco. Brecht. Pirandello. O'Casey. Western suite MCA(R) Prairie morning. Round-up. Night-herding. Buckaroo. Riding home.	12 20
SMIT, Leo Symphony No. 2 MIL(R)	18
STRINGFIELD, Lamar At evening from The Southern Mountains CF	4

	Duration (min)			Duration (min)
Mountain song from The Southern Mountains CF	4.5		WARD, Robert Hymn and celebration GAL(R)	10
STUART, Hugh Manhattan vignettes SHAW(R)	10.5		WITHORNE, Emerson Symphony No. 2 CF(R)	33
SUBOTNIK, Morton Lamentation I for orchestra and electronic sounds MCA(R)	NA			

FULL SYMPHONY ORCHESTRA WITH SOLO INSTRUMENT OR VOICE

	Solo	Duration* (min)
ADLER, Samuel Song and dance OX(R)	vla	13
BENNETT, David Concerto in G-minor CF(R)	sax	NA
DIAMOND, David Concerto No. 1 SMPC(R)	vln	25
FOSS, Lukas Concerto CF(R)	vlc	28
FULEIHAN, Anis Concerto No. 2 GS(R)	pno	21
GOULD, Morton Concerto MIL(R)	vla	20
HELPS, Robert Concerto CFP(R)	pno	NA
KLEINSINGER, George Concerto CHAP(R)	vln	14
LADERMAN, Ezra Concerto OX(R) Magic prison OX(R)	vln 2 Narr; text: from poems and letters of Emily Dickinson and the recollections of T. W. Higginson by Archibald MacLeish	27 25
LAZAROF, Henri Concerto AMP(R) Ricercar AMP(R)	vlc vla and pno	27 16

*Approximate

	Solo	Duration (min)
LEES, Benjamin		
Concerto B&H(R)	ob	16.5
Concerto B&H(R)	str qrt	22
LUKE, Ray		
Concerto OX(R)	bsn	17
MacDOWELL, Edward (H. Wiley Hitchcock, Ed.)		
Concerto No. 2 in D-minor DCP	pno	26
PERRY, Julia		
Concerto CF(R)	vln	17
PISTON, Walter		
Concerto AMP(R)	cl	15
READ, Gardner		
Fantasy, Op. 38 AMP(R)	vla	NA
RIEGGER, Wallingford		
Variations, Op. 71 AMP(R)	vln	NA
ROREM, Ned		
Concerto No. 2 SMPC(R)	pno	NA
Sun B&H(R)	high voice	26
(For contents and authors of texts, see "Solo Vocal Music")		
SCHWARTZ, Elliott		
Magic music for orchestra, piano and other sounds AB(R)	pno	13
(See also "Percussion")		
TRIMBLE, Lester		
Duo concertante CFP(R)	2 vln	18
TUTHILL, Burnet C.		
Concerto, Op. 54 KING(R)	trb	15
(See also "Band")		
WARD, Robert		
Concerto GAL(R)	pno	14

Composer, Title and Publisher	Author of Text or Libretto	Type	Acts	Voices	Duration* (min)
ARGENTO, Dominick Christopher Sly B&H(R)	John Manlove (based on Shakespeare's The Taming of the Shrew)	comedy	2 scenes and interlude	3 S, m-S, 3 T, Bar, 2 B-Bar, B	70
BARAB, Seymour Phillip Marshall TP(R)	based on Dostoevski's The Idiot	Civil War Drama	2	(not available)	120
CALDWELL, Mary E. The night of the star TP(R)	Mary E. Caldwell	drama	1	2 S, m-S, T, 2 Bar, B-Bar, Sp, ch (SSAA)	60

HITCHCOCK, H. Wiley, Ed. (NOTE: The following operas are listed as a matter of historical interest although complete information concerning the Type, Acts, Voices, and Duration is not available):

BARKER, John Nelson and John Bray: The Indian Princess DCP (the script and libretto for the first lyric drama on the story of Pocahontas and Captain John Smith)

BRISTOW, George: Rip Van Winkle (N. Y. 1882) DCP

CHADWICK, George W. Judith (N. Y. 1901) DCP (based on the Biblical heroine) Tabasco (N. Y. 1894) DCP (a combination of light opera and burlesque, including a plantation ballad)

---

*Approximate

105

Composer, Title and Publisher	Author of Text or Libretto	Type	Acts	Voices	Duration (min)
HOVHANESS, Alan The leper king, Op. 219 CFP(R)	Alan Hovhaness	dance drama	1	8 Bar (or any multiple of 8) or 8 m-S (or any multiple of 8) and 8 Bar (or any multiple of 8)	33
MAYER, William Brief candle TP(R)	Milton Feist	drama	1	mime and ch	6
MOORE, Douglas Carry Nation GAL(R)	William North Jayme	drama	Prologue and 7 scenes	5 S, boy S, m-S, 3 T, 5 Bar, B-Bar, ch, dancers	120
WEISGALL, Hugo Nine rivers from Jordan TP(R) (libretto only available)	Dennis Johnston	drama	Prologue and 3 acts	3 (or 1) S, m-S, 2 T, 2 Bar, B-Bar, B, 20 secondary male roles, ch	120
WESTERGAARD, Peter Mr. and Mrs. Discobbolos AB(R)	Edward Lear	comedy	1	S, T	17

8. BAND
(Including Wind Symphony)

Duration* (min) / Duration (min)

ADLER, Samuel
Festive prelude   MIL   7

AITKEN, Hugh
Four quiet pieces   EV   4
  Arioso. Chorale.
  Canon. Song.
Partita for band   OX   4.5

BARBER, Samuel
Intermezzo from <u>Vanessa</u>   4
GS

BEGLARIAN, Grant
A hymn for our times EBM 14
  (for 3 bands. The
  original 6-band version
  is available on rental.)

BENNETT, David
Saxophone royal (solo sax)   5
SMC

BENNETT, Robert Russell
Down to the sea in ships   12.5
W-7
  1. The way of a ship
  2. Mists and mystery
  3. Songs in the salty air
  4. Waltz of the clipper
  ships
  5. Finale, introducing
  the S. S. Eagle March

BENSON, Warren
Concertino for saxophone   NA**
  and band   MCA
Helix (a concerto for tuba   14
  and wind ensemble) MCA
The mask of night   MCA   NA
Night song   CHAP   6.5
  (a nocturne)

Recuerdo   MCA   NA
  (with oboe and English
  horn solos)
Staredge for saxophone   17
  and band   MCA

BERKOWITZ, Leonard
Divertimento for sym-   5.5
  phonic winds   CF
Toccata, theme and   13
  variations   CF

BERKOWITZ, Sol
Paradigm (a jazz adven-   5
  ture in sonata allegro
  form)   FM

BIELAWA, Herbert
Concert fanfare   SHAW   4
Spectrum (for tape re-   6
  corder and band)   SHAW

BROWN, Rayner
Concertino for piano and   14
  band   WIM

BROWN, Thomas
Pattern percussion for   NA
  tom-tom, snare drum,
  bongos, bass drum, and
  timp and band   KMI
  (See also "Percussion")
Percussionata for percus- NA
  sion ensemble and band
  KMI
  (See also "Percussion")

BULLARD, Bob
Tahquamenon   KMI   6

---

*Approximate
**In a few instances, the timings in minutes for the band works were
  not indicated in the scores or from information received from the
  publishers. In those cases, the symbol "NA" is used.

	Duration (min)		Duration (min)

CACAVAS, John
  Burnished brass CF — 2.5
  Ceremonial prelude FM — 2.5
  Dynamarch EBM — 3
  Fanfares for the New Year CF — 2
  Midnight soliloquy (with saxophone quartet, or trio or solo) EBM — 3.5
  Overture concertante BI — 3.5
  Parada Española (concert march) CHAP — 5
  Rhapsodic essay CF — 3
  7 fanfares for the marching winds CF — 2
  Streets of Athens CF — 2.5

CARTER, Charles
  Dance and intermezzo CLB — 5.5
  Overture in classical style B&H — 4
  Queen city suite BI — 9
    Fanfare and processional. Grass roots. Harvest jubilee.
  Sonata for winds CLB — 4
  Three pieces in antique style CF — 4
    Little canon. Madrigal. Motet.

CHANCE, John Barnes
  Blue lake, an overture B&H — 4

COKER, Wilson
  Polyphonic ode TP — 5.5

CONLEY, Lloyd
  Quiet valley KMI — 3.5
  A symphonic invention KMI — 6

COPLAND, Aaron
  The red pony (film suite for band) B&H(R) — 15
    1. a. Dream march
       b. Circus music
    2. Walk to the bunk house
    3. Grandfather's story
    4. Happy ending

CRESTON, Paul
  Anatolia (Turkish rhapsody) SHAW — 8

CROLEY, Randell
  Song of my youth (with optional speaker; text: after the poem of Ishikawa Takuboku) JBI — 12

DEDRICK, Art
  Design for autumn KMI — 3

DELLO JOIO, Norman
  Fantasies on a theme by Haydn EBM(R) — 14
  Songs of Abelard EBM(R) — NA

DIEMER, Emma Lou
  The brass menagerie MIL — 7

DIERCKS, John
  Concertino for oboe and band TP(R) — 8.5

DILLON, Robert M.
  Four winds (overture) CLB — 3
  Southwestern panorama SHAW Rangeland. Forest of steel. Desert. Roundup. — 9
  Three themes for band SHAW — 5

DONATO, Anthony
  Concert overture EBM(R) — 8

EDMONDSON, John B.
  Hymn and postlude KMI — 3.5

EFFINGER, Cecil
  Prelude and fugue EV — 7

ELKUS, Jonathan
  "Camino Real" TP(R) — 8

ERB, Donald
  Compendium FM — 5
  Space music FM — 3
  Stargazing (for band and electronic tape) TP — 3
    I. The stars come out
    II. Comets, meteors, shooting stars
    III. The surface of the sun

Band (Including Wind Symphony)   109

	Duration (min)
ERICKSON, Frank	
Chorale for band CF	3.5
Concerto for saxophone	NA
and band BI	
Earth-song GS	8
Royal armada CF	4.5
Steel and glass AMC	4
FELDSTEIN, Saul	
Timetable (featuring drum-	4
set solo) AMC	
(See also "Percussion")	
FRACKENPOHL, Arthur	
Diversion in F SHAW	3.5
On the go SHAW	1.5
FRANK, Marcel G.	
Pas de deux (ballet di-	3.5
vertissement for band) BI	
FROCK, George and John	
Warrington	
Drums of America TP	3.5
(See also "Percussion")	
GATES, George	
La contessa SMC	4
Mosaico de Mexico (suite)	7.5
SMC	
I. Alma llanera	
II. Azteca (Subo Subo)	
III. Huapango (de Veracruz)	
GILLIS, Don	
Ballet for band SMC	13
Lone star (Rhapsody for	10
band) SMC	
Saga of a pioneer SMC	23
1. The land beyond	
2. The pioneers	
3. Song of memory	
4. Centennial celebration	
GORDON, Louis	
Man and machine COL	6.5
GORDON, Philip	
Andante for band BI	4
Appalachian fantasy W-7	4
Canticle for band MIL	1.5
Canzona for band MIL	4
Elizabethan suite W-7	4
Invocation MIL	4
Sierra spectrum MIL	4.5
Sonnet for band BI	5
Three modern chorales BI	6

	Duration (min)
GOULD, Morton	
Hillbilly CF	2
Rumbolero CF	4
GROSS, Charles	
Black-eyed Susie CF	3
GRUNDMAN, Clare	
American folk rhapsody	5
No. 3 B&H	
Dance and interlude B&H	3.5
English suite B&H	9
The oak and the ash.	
Barb'ra Allen (old tune).	
The girl I left behind me	
(old English).	
The British grenadiers	
(16th century).	
Japanese rhapsody B&H	5
Three sketches for winds	5
B&H Carousel.	
Charade. Callithump.	
A Welsh rhapsody B&H	5
Jenny Jones. To town	
with Deio. Two hearts.	
HADDAD, Don	
Adagio and allegro for	7
horn and band SHAW	
HARTLEY, Walter S.	
Concertino for trumpet	NA
and wind ensemble JBI	
Concertino for tuba and	NA
wind ensemble TP	
Concerto for 3 trombones	NA
and band CF	
HAUFRECHT, Herbert	
Prelude to a tragedy BI	NA
HEISINGER, Brent	
Soliloquy for band SHAW	3.5
HENDERSON, Kenneth	
The lancers KMI	4
Trade winds KMI	2
HITCHCOCK, H. Wiley, Ed.	
Cotillions and country	varies
dances DCP	
Dances of the Civil War	varies
era DCP	

	Duration (min)
HOGG, Merle E.	
Suite for band SHAW	11
Introduction. Folk song.	
Carnival. Ballad. Dance.	
HOSMER, L.	
Southern rhapsody CF	10
HOVHANESS, Alan	
Hymn to Yerevan AB	4
Suite for band CFP(R)	10
Aria. Processional.	
Aria. Canzona. Aria.	
Processional.	
Tapor No. 1 (Processional	5
for band) CFP(R)	
Three journeys to a holy	27
mountain (Symphony No.	
20) AB(R)	
HOWARD, Dean C.	
Elegy for moderns KMI	3
JENKINS, Joseph Willcox	
Cuernavaca COL	4
JOHNSTON, Jack	
Games for band EV	7
Pastorale. Chase. War.	
Excursion.	
JONES, Robert W.	
Toccanta concertante SHAW	7.5
KECHLEY, Gerald	
Antiphony for winds CF	5
KAY, Hershy	
Cakewalk suite B&H(R)	13
Grand walkaround. Wall-	
flower waltz. Sleight of	
feet. Entrance of the magi-	
cians. Gala cakewalk.	
Deck the halls with boughs	2
of holly (a merrie fugue)	
B&H	
Pat-a-pan (a fantasy) B&H	4
Variations on "Joy to the	3
world" B&H	
KLEINSINGER, George	
Symphony of winds (with	14
narrator; text by com-	
poser) CFP(R)	

	Duration (min)
KORTE, Karl	
Ceremonial prelude and	9
passacaglia CF(R)	
KOSTECK, Gregory	
Elegy for band BI	4
Requiem for trombone	4
and band BI	
KOUTZEN, Boris	
Rhapsody for symphonic	13
band GEN(R)	
KROEGER, Karl	
Declaration for trumpet	4
and band TP	
LATHAM, William	
Brighton Beach S-B	3
Dodecaphonic set CLB	4
LEE, Dai-Keong	
Prelude and hula COL	5
LOGAN, Robert	
Presto chango (solo horn,	5
clarinet, saxophone,	
cornet with band) TP	
LUKE, Ray	
Prelude and march LMP	4
MADDEN, Edward J.	
A fantasia on a folk	6
theme COL	
MAILMAN, Martin	
Alarums MIL	5
Overture for band MIL	5.5
Partita MIL	10
The whalemen's chorale	NA
(with optional SATB	
chorus; text: Herman	
Melville) MIL(R)	
MALTBY, Richard	
Ballad for brass and per-	3
cussion CF	
(See also "Percussion")	
Blues essay for trumpet	3
or horn and band EBM	
Jazz waltz CF	4

		Duration (min)

McBETH, W. Francis
Chant and jubilo   SMC   8
Joyant narrative   SMC   4
Masque   SMC   7
Mosaic   SMC   8
Second suite for band SMC   10
Gigue. Dirge. Entry.

MITCHELL, Rex
Panorama for band (a sym-   7.5
phonic portrait of
Americana)   EBM

MORRISSEY, John J.
Bravura for trumpets and   3
band   EBM
Elegy for band   FM   5
Medieval suite   MIL   NA
Royal procession   EBM   5

MURRAY, Lyn
Collage for clarinet and   20
band   WIM

NELSON, Ron
Alleluia, July 20, 1969 B&H   3
Elegy   B&H   4
Guide to the elements of   NA
music   B&H
Meditation on the syllable   NA
OM   B&H
Rocky Point holiday   B&H   5.5
Trilogy: - JFK - MLK -   NA
RFK   B&H

NESTICO, Sammy
Horizons west   KMI   5

OTT, Joseph
Mini laude   CBP   6

PEARSON, Robert
Caprice   SHAW   4
Concert piece for winds   8
and percussion SHAW
(See also "Percussion")
Minuteman   SHAW   3
Watergate   SHAW   3

PHILLIPS, Peter
Gothic suite   OX   7
Round/trip (a divertimento   5
for band)   BI

POWELL, Mel
Capriccio   SHAW   6

		Duration (min)

PRESSER, William
Capriccio for tuba and   5.5
band   TP

PYLE, Francis Johnson
Far dominion   LPI   7

RALEIGH, S.
Maledictions for band COL   NA

RAPHLING, Sam
Involvement   BI   4

READ, Gardner
Dunlap's Creek   COL   NA

RECK, David
Summer festival   TP   7
Fanfare. March.
Chorale. Song.

REED, Alfred
Ballade for saxophone   5
and band   SMC
Chorale prelude in E-   5
minor   SMC
A festive overture   FM   7
Intrada drammatica EBM   5
The music makers (a   4
concert overture) FM
Seascape (a dramatic in-   4.5
termezzo for baritone or
trombone and band) EBM
Wapawekka (white sands)   6
(a symphonic rhapsody
on Canadian Indian
themes)   EBM

REED, H. Owen
Theme and variations MIL   8.5

RHODES, Philip
Three pieces for band COL   NA

RICHARDS, Johnny
Don Camillo   AMP   6

SACCO, P. Peter
Atlantis (the lost continent) 12
(a suite in 4 parts) CF(R)
1. Nocturne and morning
hymn of praise
2. A court function
3. "I love thee" (the
Prince and Aana)
4. The destruction of
Atlantis

Duration (min)

SPEARS, Jared

Don Quixote (suite) CF(R)   12
1. Spanish village
2. Sancho Panza
3. Dulcinea
4. Don Quixote
Pass in review   CF   2
Suite   WIM   8

SAYLOR, Richard
Ballata   KMI   5.5

SCHAEFER, Willis H.
Ballada   FM   3.5

SCHMIDT, William
The Natchez trace   WIM   4
Sakura variations   WIM   10
Variations on a Negro   10
folk song   WIM

SCHUMAN, William
Dedication fanfare   TP   4.5
Variations on "America"   7
(based on a piece for
organ by Charles Ives)
TP(R)

SIEGMEISTER, Elie
Western suite   MCA(R)   20
(for contents, see "Full
Symphony Orchestra")

SIENNICKI, Edmund J.
Scherzo   EV   3.5

SKOLNIK, Walter
Chorale fantasia   EV   4
Toccata festiva   EV   4

SMITH, Julia and Cecile Vashaw
Remember the Alamo! (with   12.5
narrator and optional SATB
chorus; text: Lt. Col.
William Barret Travis)
TP(R)

SMITH, Julia
Sails aloft (an overture)   7
TP(R)

SOUSA, John Philip (H. Wiley
Hitchcock, Ed.)
The Sousa march folio   varies
(Cincinnati, 1902) DCP

Duration (min)

SPEARS, Jared
Three cameos for band   4
CPC

STARER, Robert
Fanfaronade for band MCA   3
Reverie for trumpet and   3
band   SF

STAUFFER, Donald
Moods modal   KMI   4.5

THIELMAN, Ronald
Chelsea suite   LMP   5
Overture odalisque   BI   4

TUBB, Monte
Concert piece for band TP   5.5

TULL, Fisher
Toccata for band   B&H   5

TURNER, Godfrey
Fanfare, chorale and   9
finale   B&H(R)

TUTHILL, Burnet C.
Concerto for clarinet and   15
band, Op. 28 EV(R)
Concerto for trombone and   15
band, Op. 54   KING
(See also "Full Symphony
Orchestra")
Overture for symphonic   9
band, Op. 19   EV

VELKE, Fritz
Plaything   SHAW   7

WAGNER, Joseph
Concerto grosso for sym-   14
phonic band   W-7
Overture "American   6
Jubilee"   W-7
Symphonic transitions for   9
concert band   MIL(R)

WALKER, Richard
The Corybantes   KMI   6

WARD, Robert
Fiesta processional GAL   4.5

WASHBURN, Robert
Overture: Sunmount   OX   4.5
Suite for band   OX   12.5

	Duration (min)	Duration (min)

WEINER, Lawrence
Atropos   LMP   4.5
Daedalic symphony (1st   6
   movement, allegro) SHAW

WEISS, Edward
Tania   S-B   2

WERLE, Floyd E.
Concertino for trumpet,   7
   trombone, tuba and
   band BI
   I. Vintage foxtrot
   II. Lullaby
   III. Greek dance

WHEAR, Paul W.
Introduction and invention   4
   LMP
Jedermann   LMP   4
Land of Lincoln (march)   4.5
   LMP
Modal miniatures   LMP   4
Sonata for band   LMP   6
Wycliffe variations   LMP   9.5

WHITE, Donald H.
Ambrosian hymn variants   6
   (Aeterna Christi munera)
   EV
Introduction and allegro   5
   LMP
Patterns   EV   NA
Terpsimetrics   SHAW   5

WILLIAMS, Clifton
Concertino for percussion   8
   and band   S-B
   (See also "Percussion")
from "Symphonic dances" SF NA
   No. 2   Cotillion
   No. 3   Fiesta
   No. 5   New generation
The patriots   AMC   4.5
Trail scenes suite   SF   NA
   Roundup. Nighthawk.
   Railheads.
Trilogy - suite in 3 move-   10
   ments   SMC

WILLIS, Richard
Aria and toccata   MIL   4

1. VOICE

SOLO VOCAL MUSIC (Piano accompaniment unless otherwise indicated)

Composer, Title and Publisher	Range	Author of Text
BECK, John Ness		
Song of joy CFP	med	Biblical
GRIFFES, Charles		
Four German songs CFP	med, high	trans: Donna K. Anderson
At last I hold you		E. Geibel
Calm sea		Goethe
They buried him at the crossroads		Heinrich Heine
To the wind		N. Lenau
Four impressions CFP	med, high	Oscar Wilde
Dawn. Early morning in London. The garden. The sea.		
LEICHTLING, Alan		
Canticle 1, Op. 51 (with flute obb) SEM	high	Biblical
Eleven songs from "A Shropshire Lad" (with chamber ensemble) SEM	T	A. E. Housman
Psalm 37, Op. 39 (with harp, piano, 4 percussion, string quartet) SEM	m-S	Biblical
Three songs by Emily Dickinson (with cello) SEM	Bar	Emily Dickinson
Trial and death of Socrates (with clarinet, flute, harp) SEM	med male voice	Socrates
Two proverbs (with clarinet trio) SEM	m-S	Biblical
ROREM, Ned		
War scenes (a cycle) B&H	Bar	Walt Whitman
SIEGMEISTER, Elie		
Madam to you SEM	S	Langston Hughes
STEINER, Gitta		
Concert piece for seven No. 1 (with 2 percussionists, flute, piano, cello) SEM	S	Gitta Steiner
Concert piece for seven No. 2 (with 2 percussionists, flute, double bass, piano) SEM	S	Gitta Steiner
Interludes (with vibraphone) SEM	med	Gitta Steiner

Composer, Title and Publisher	Range	Author of Text
Pages from a summer journal SEM	med	Gitta Steiner
Three songs by James Joyce SEM	med	James Joyce
Three poems (with 2 percussionists) SEM	med	Gitta Steiner
Two songs SEM	med	Gitta Steiner

SYDEMAN, William

Composition (with string quartet and tape(R)) OKM	T	William Sydeman
Malediction (with string quartet and tape(R)) OKM	T	William Sydeman

MIXED CHORUS (SATB a cappella unless otherwise indicated)

Composer, Title and Publisher	Chorus	Solos	Accompaniment	Author of Text
BEESON, Jack				
To a lady who asked for a cypher (a chromatic double canon) B&H				Anon
BEVERIDGE, Thomas				
Once (a cantata in memoriam for Dr. Martin Luther King, Jr.) SHAW		S, Narr	org and opt brass and perc	Latin Mass for the Dead, Union Prayer Book of Jewish Worship, Rabindranath Tagore, James Russell Lowell, trad spirituals
BLANK, Allan				
The frogs OKM	SSAATTBB			Aristophones
BOATWRIGHT, Howard				
We sing of God, the mighty source ECS			org	Christopher Smart, 1765
BRUBECK, Dave				
The gates of justice (a cantata) SHAW		T, B-Bar (solos)	11-piece brass ensemble, 2 perc, jazz trio (R)	text adapted by Dave and Iola Brubeck from the Jewish Bible, Union Prayer Book of Reform Judaism, teachings of Dr. Martin Luther King, Jr.
BURROUGHS, Bob				
The gift of life (a motet) BI				Bob Burroughs

Composer, Title and Publisher	Chorus	Solos	Accompaniment	Author of Text
The Knight of Bethlehem (a contemporary setting) BI			pno (with opt ob)	adapted by Bob Burroughs
Seven psalms for contemporary living BI			brass ensemble and org	Biblical; paraphrased by Kenneth N. Taylor
CHIHARA, Paul				
The 90th Psalm SHAW	SSSAAA TTTBBB			Biblical
COHEN, Michael				
If I should learn BI			pno	Edna St. Vincent Millay
CRAWFORD, John				
Two madrigals ECS Cherry-ripe. To daisies, not to shut so soon (SAATB)				Robert Herrick
DIEMENTE, Edward				
Three motets SEM			org	from Latin texts
Two pieces for mixed chorus SEM Sparrow				Elizabeth Randall-Smith
We sat on the mountain's back				Kathleen Lombardo
EARLS, Paul				
Out of the depths ECS (Psalm 130)			org	Biblical
ERICKSON, Robert				
Down at Piraeus OKM			pre-recorded tape (R)	Plato
FELCIANO, Richard				
Words of Saint Peter WLP			org & electronic tape	Biblical
HEUSSENSTAMM, George				
Poem of circumstance SEM				Jean Cocteau
IVES, Charles				
Psalm 90 (Edited by John Kirkpatrick and Gregg Smith) TP			org and bells	Biblical
KIRK, Theron				
Four seasons songs B&H			fl, c-b, opt	
1. Now welcome summer				Geoffrey Chaucer
2. To autumn				John Keats
3. Winter				Shakespeare
4. Spring				Thomas Nashe

Composer, Title and Publisher	Chorus	Solos	Accompani- ment	Author of Text
Song of the dance (Cantar de baile) SHAW			pno	sung entirely on rhythmic
LA MONTAINE, John				syllables
Erode the Great PJS			orch(R)	text adapted by John La Montaine
The Shephardes playe PJS			orch(R)	text adapted from the early English play by John La Montaine
LEVY, Frank				
This is my letter to the world SEM				Emily Dickin- son
McAFEE, Don				
Corinthians on love BI				Biblical
Graffiti BI				text adapted by Don McAfee
I will lift up mine eyes (Psalm 121) BI	unison		pno or org	Biblical
The morning times: a madrigal for tomorrow morning's breakfast BI				text adapted by Don McAfee
MECHEM, Kirke				
Zorabel (chamber cantata) ECS		S, T, Bar, B	wind quintet, str quintet, pno(R)	text adapted by Kirke Mechem
PFAUTSCH, Lloyd				
I hear America singing SHAW			pno	Walt Whitman
PINKHAM, Daniel				
In the beginning of creation ECS			electronic tape, acc	Biblical
Mass of the good Shepherd ECS Threefold Kyrie eleison. Ninefold Kyrie eleison. Trisagion. Gloria in excelsis. Sanctus. Benedictus qui venit. Agnus Dei. The anthem.	unison		org	liturgical
RAFFMAN, Relly				
Matins ECS				George Herbert
REIF, Paul				
Triple city SEM			brass ensemble	William J. Grace

Composer, Title and Publisher	Chorus	Solos	Accompaniment	Author of Text
SCHRAMM, Harold Canticle (an aleatory setting) BI				Harold Schramm
SILVER, Frederick Before the paling of the stars (a rock setting) BI			pno	Christina Rossetti
SPENCER, Williametta Death be not proud SHAW				John Donne
STEINER, Gitta Four choruses of Emily Dickinson SEM I have no life but this. I'm nobody. Our share of night to bear. Summer for thee. (above published separately)				Emily Dickin- son
WOOLF, Gregory Mass WLP Kyrie. Sanctus. Gloria. Angus Dei.	SSSSAAAA TTTTBBBB		electronic tape and org	liturgical

WOMEN'S CHORUS (SSA a cappella unless otherwise indicated)

CRAWFORD, John
Three Shakespeare songs
ECS
1. Tell me where is
   fancy bred
2. Come away, death
3. It was a lover and
   his lass
			pno or 11
			solo instr:
			fl, ob, cl,
			bsn, hn, timp
			(in no. 2 & 3
			only), str
			quintet
				Shakespeare

SYDEMAN, William Prometheus (a cantata) OKM		3 male soli	orch(R)	Aeschylus

MEN'S CHORUS (TTBB a cappella unless otherwise indicated)

GOLDSTEIN, William I sit and look out SHAW			pno	Walt Whitman
HEUSSENSTAMM, George Dirge in the woods SEM				George Meredith

CHORUS WITH INSTRUMENTAL (OR ELECTRONIC) ACCOMPANIMENT

Composer, Title and Publisher	Chorus	Solos	Accompaniment	Author of Text	Duration (min)
BEVERIDGE, Thomas Once (a cantata in memoriam for Dr. Martin Luther King, Jr.) SHAW	SATB	S, Narr	org and opt brass and perc	trad spirituals, Latin Mass for the Dead, Union Prayer Book of Jewish Worship, Rabindranath Tagore, James Russell Lowell	40
BRUBECK, Dave The gates of justice (a cantata) SHAW(R)	SATB	T, B-Bar	11-piece brass ensemble, 2 perc, jazz trio	text adapted by Dave and Iola Brubeck from the Jewish Bible, Union Prayerbook of Reform Judaism, teachings of Dr. Martin Luther King, Jr.	70
CRAWFORD, John Three Shakespeare songs ECS (for contents, see "Women's Chorus")	SSA		pno or 11 solo instr: fl, ob, cl, bsn, timp, str quintet	Shakespeare	6
ERICKSON, Robert Down at Piraeus OKM(R)	SATB		pre-recorded tape	Plato	5
FELCIANO, Richard Words of Saint Peter WLP	SATB		org & electronic tape	Biblical	NA
LA MONTAINE, John Erode the Great PJS(R)	SATB		full	adapted by John La Montaine	90
The shephardes playe PJS(R)	SATB		full	adapted from the early English play by John La Montaine	60
MECHEM, Kirke Zorabel (chamber cantata) ECS(R)	SATB	S, T, Bar, B	wind quintet, str quintet, pno	text adapted by Kirke Mechem	NA
REIF, Paul Triple city SEM	SATB		brass ensemble	William J. Grace	NA
SYDEMAN, William Prometheus (cantata) OKM(R)	SSA	3 male soli	full	Aeschylus	NA

Composer, Title and Publisher	Chorus	Solos	Accompaniment	Author of Text	Duration (min)

WOOLF, Gregory
  Mass WLP
  Kyrie. Sanctus.
  Gloria. Agnus Dei.
	SSSSAAAA
	TTTTBBBB
			org & electronic tape	liturgical	5

2. INSTRUMENTAL SOLO

KEYBOARD MUSIC

PIANO, TWO HANDS (including harpsichord)

BENSON, Warren
  Three Macedonian miniatures B&H

COPLAND, Aaron
  Salón México (arr by composer)
  B&H

COWELL, Henry
  Hilarious curtain opener and
    ritornelle   TP
  Maestoso   TP

DIEMER, Emma Lou
  Gavotte   B&H
  Gigue   B&H
  Invention   B&H

DUKELSKY, Vladimir (Vernon Duke)
  Zephire et Flore   B&H

FAITH, Richard
  The dark riders (toccata) SHAW
  Sonata No. 1   SHAW

FINE, Irving
  Homage à Mozart   B&H

FULEIHAN, Anis
  Ionian pentagon   B&H
  Sonata No. 9   SMPC
  Sonata No. 14   B&H

GARLICK, Antony
  Three pieces for piano   SEM

KUPFERMAN, Meyer
  14 canonic inventions   GEN

LEWIS, Robert Hall
  Five movements for piano   SEM

MUCZYNSKI, Robert
  Tocatta   GS

MARTINO, Donald
  Piano fantasy   ECS

MILLER, Jesse
  Five movements for piano   SEM

RAPHLING, Sam
  Six indiscretions   GEN

RUSSELL, Robert
  Places (a suite)   GEN

ROVICS, Howard
  Three studies for piano   OKM

STEINER, Gitta
  Fantasy piece for piano   SEM
  Sonata   SEM
  Three pieces for piano   SEM
  Trio (with 2 percussionists) SEM
    (see also "Percussion")

SYDEMAN, William
  Fantasy piece for harpsichord OKM
  Three pieces and finale for piano
    and tape(R)   OKM

ORGAN

KOPP, Frederick
  Passacaglia in the olden style SEM

STRING MUSIC (with piano unless otherwise indicated)

VIOLIN

BLANK, Allan
Music for violin solo   OKM

DE BERADINIS, John
Dialogues for violin and per-
cussion   SEM
(See also "Percussion")

GARLICK, Antony
Sonata   SEM

HEUSSENSTAMM, George
Micron (unacc)   SEM

LEWIS, Robert Hall
Sonata (unacc)   SEM

STEINER, Gitta
Refractions (unacc)   SEM

SYDEMAN, William
Duo   OKM
Projections I for amplified
violin and tape (R)   OKM
Sonata (unacc)   OKM
Variations   OKM

VIOLA

BLANK, Allan
Song of ascents (unacc)   OKM

VIOLONCELLO

SYDEMAN, William
Duo   OKM

DOUBLE BASS

SYDEMAN, William
Song   OKM

HARP

POLIN, Claire
Summer settings   LM

GUITAR

SYDEMAN, William
Fantasy for guitar   OKM

SHAUGHNESSY, Robert
Duo for recorder (or flute or
violin) and guitar   SEM

WOODWIND MUSIC (with piano unless
otherwise indicated)

FLUTE

BENNETT, David
Flute royale   CLB

HEUSSENSTAMM, George
Windgate (unacc)   SEM

KOPP, Frederick
Portrait of a woman   SEM

PLESKOW, Raoul
Two pieces for flute   SEM

REIF, Paul
Banter   SEM

ROVICS, Howard
Cybernetic study No. 1   OKM

SHAUGHNESSY, Robert
Paradigm (unacc)   SEM

STEINER, Gitta
Jouissance   SEM

SYDEMAN, William
Duo   OKM

OBOE

BLANK, Allan
Moments in time   OKM

REYNOLDS, Verne
Three elegies   MCA

CLARINET

FRACKENPOHL, Arthur
Sonatina   GS

GARLICK, Antony
Concert piece   SEM
Sonata   SEM

Addendum to Supplement

HEUSSENSTAMM, George
Die Jugend (unacc) SEM
Double solo for clarinet and
   percussion   SEM
   (see also "Percussion")

HODKINSON, Sydney
Drawings: set No. 3 (with
   drums)   MP
   (see also "Percussion")

KRAFT, Leo
Five pieces   GEN

LEVY, Frank
Sonata   SEM

RUSSELL, Robert
Scherzo   GEN

STEINER, Gitta
Fantasy   SEM

SYDEMAN, William
Piece for clarinet and tape(R)
   OKM

SAXOPHONE

DIEMENTE, Edward
Response   SEM

NOTT, Douglas
Rhapsodic song   SHAW

SNYDER, Randall
Sonata   TP

BASSOON

LEVY, Frank
Sonata   SEM

RECORDER

SHAUGHNESSY, Robert
Duo for recorder (or flute or
   violin) and guitar   SEM

BRASS MUSIC (with piano unless
   otherwise indicated)

TRUMPET

CUSTER, Arthur
Rondo   GEN

DIEMENTE, Edward
Something else (with pre-recorded
   tape (R)   SEM

SYDEMAN, William
Duo for trumpet and percussion
   OKM   (see also "Percussion")

FRENCH HORN

EFFINGER, Cecil
Rondino   GS

HUTCHINSON, Warner
Hornpiece 1 (with tape(R))   SEM

SYDEMAN, William
Concert piece (with organ)   OKM
   (also with string orchestra
   acc(R))
Duo for horn and piano   OKM

TROMBONE

STEINER, Gitta
Five pieces   SEM

TUBA

PRESSER, William
Rondo   CLB

3. INSTRUMENTAL ENSEMBLES

STRING ENSEMBLES

DUOS AND TRIOS

HEUSSENSTAMM, George
Canonograph No. 2   3 str instr
  SEM
String trio SEM   vln, vla,
                          vlc
Tre celli   SEM   3 vlc

LEVY, Frank
Duo for two violins   2 vln
  SEM

SHAUGHNESSY, Robert
Duo for violin and   vln, gtr
  guitar   SEM

STEINER, Gitta
String trio SEM   vln, vla,
                          vlc

SYDEMAN, William
A cello trio OKM   3 vlc (2
                          parts pre-
                          recorded,
                          available
                          on rental)
Encounters OKM   vln, vlc,
                          pno
Haus Musik OKM   vln, vla,
                          vlc
Trio OKM   3 c-b
Trio OKM   vln, vla,
                          pno
Trio for treble in-   3 treble
  struments OKM   instr

QUARTETS (2 vln, vla, vlc unless
  otherwise indicated)

DANKNER, Stephen
String quartet SEM

GARLICK, Antony
String quartet No. 1 SEM
String quartet No. 2 SEM

HEUSSENSTAMM, George
String quartet   SEM

KOPP, Frederick
Passacaglia in the olden style
  for string quartet SEM

LEICHTLING, Alan
Quartet   SEM

LEVY, Frank
String quartet   SEM

LEWIS, Robert Hall
First string quartet SEM
Second string quartet SEM

MILLER, Jesse
String quartet SEM

SELETSKY, Harold
String quartet, Op. 8 OKM

STEINER, Gitta
String quartet SEM

SYDEMAN, William
Quartet for strings No. 2 OKM

STRINGS WITH VOICE AND/ OR
WINDS, PERCUSSION

BLANK, Allan
Music for three players 3 treble instr
  OKM
Variations   OKM   cl, vla

BROWN, Rayner
Concertino WIM   hp, brass
                          quintet

CARTER, Elliott
Pastorale TP   pno, vla, E-
                          hn (or cl)

DELP, Ron
Dreams, 1970 SEM   fl, cl, c-b,
(see also "Percussion")   4 perc

DIEMENTE, Edward
Quartet SEM   fl, cl, vib,
                          c-b
Quartet SEM   sax, trb, c-
                          b, perc
(see also "Percussion")
3-31- '70 SEM   trp, trb, sax,
                          elec. gtr,
                          elec. bass,
                          dr, voice
Unvelopment SEM   c-b(solo), 3
                          sax, elec.
                          gtr, cel, 2
                          perc
(see also "Percussion")

HEUSSENSTAMM, George
Mini-variations SEM — fl, ob, vln, vla, vlc
Trio SEM — cl, vln, vlc

KERR, Harrison
Notations on a sensitized plate TP — voice, cl, str qrt, pno

LEVY, Frank
Dialogue SEM — tba, hp, timp, str

LUTI, Vincent F.
Mixed quintet BCM — fl, cl, vln, vlc, pno

OLIVEROS, Pauline
Aeolian partitions BCM — fl, cl, vln, vlc, pno

PETERSON, Wayne
Phantasmagoria SEM — fl, cl, c-b

PLESKOW, Raoul
Movement SEM — fl, vlc, pno
Three bagatelles SEM — c-b, fl, cl, vib

REYNOLDS, Roger
Traces CFP — pno, fl, vlc, signal generator, ring modulator, 6 channels of taped sound (taped sounds supplied with rental materials)

SWICKARD, Ralph
Four duets SEM — fl, vla

SYDEMAN, William
Divertimento OKM — fl, cl, bsn, str qrt
Double concerto OKM (see also "Band") — trp, trb, band, str
Duo for flute and double bass OKM — fl, c-b
Duo for trumpet and amplified double bass OKM — fl, amplified c-b
Fantasy and two epilogues OKM — fl, vlc, pno
Haus Musik OKM — fl, vln, vlc, pno

Quartet OKM — vln, cl, trp, c-b
Quartet OKM — vln, fl, cl, pno
Quartet OKM — ob, vln, vla, vlc
Quintet OKM — cl, hn (or trb), pno, c-b, perc
(see also "Percussion")
Trio for treble instruments OKM
Trio OKM — fl, c-b, perc
(See also "Percussion")
Trio OKM — vln, cl, c-b
Study for two flutes and piano OKM — 2 fl, pno

WOLFF, Christian
For 1, 2 or 3 people CFP — any instr or combinations

WOODWIND ENSEMBLES

DUOS AND TRIOS

DIEMENTE, Edward
Three pieces for two clarinets SEM — 2 cl

GARLICK, Antony
Two trios for three clarinets SEM — 3 cl

HEUSSENSTAMM, George
Ambages SEM — fl, cl
Canonograph No. 1 SEM — 3 woodwinds (high, med, low)

HOVHANESS, Alan
The spirit of ink, Op. 230 CFP — 3 fl
1. Apparition of the eternal one
2. Sunrise birds
3. Salutation of dawn
4. Tree of birds
5. Apparition of a celestial city
6. Strange birds
7. Angelic salutation
8. Birds in a magic forest
9. Birds amid celestial towers

KRAFT, Leo
Short suite   GEN   fl, cl, bsn

RUSSELL, Robert
Abstract No. 1 GEN   2 cl

STEINER, Gitta
Suite   SEM   fl, cl, bsn

SYDEMAN, William
Trio for treble
instruments   OKM

QUARTETS, QUINTETS AND LARGER
ENSEMBLES

DIEMENTE, Edward
Celebration for wind   instr not
ensemble SEM   available

KOPP, Frederick
Passacaglia in the olden
style for woodwind
quintet   SEM
Three movements for
woodwind quintet SEM

HEUSSENSTAMM, George
Callichoreo for wood-
wind quartet   SEM
Instabilities for wood-
wind quintet   SEM

KINGMAN, Dan
Four miniatures for
woodwind quartet WIM

LEICHTLING, Alan
Quintet No. 3 for wood-
winds   SEM

PETERSON, Wayne
Metamorphoses for
woodwind quintet SEM

REIF, Paul
Kleidoscope for wood-
wind quintet and
voice (text: Paul
Reif)   SEM

SYDEMAN, William
Texture studies for
woodwind quintet OKM
Woodwind quintet No. 1
OKM

MIXED WOODWINDS, BRASS, VOICE,
KEYBOARD, AND/OR PERCUSSION

CAMPO, Frank
Concertino WIM   3 cl, pno

DIEMENTE, Edward
Trio   SEM   fl, trp,
(see also "Percussion") perc

DRUCKMAN, Jacob
Incenters for 13 in-   instr not
struments MCA   available

MACERO, Teo
Canzona No. 1 TP   4 sax, trp

MILLER, Jesse
Settignano SEM   trp, fl, ob,
bsn, cl

ROVICS, Howard
Cybernetic study   cl, bsn,
No. 2   OKM   pno

SCHMIDT, William
Concertino   WIM   pno, brass
quintet

SYDEMAN, William
Duo   OKM   hn, b-cl
Trio   OKM   bsn, cl, pno

BRASS ENSEMBLES

DUOS, TRIOS, QUARTETS, QUINTETS
AND LARGER COMBINATIONS

ALEXANDER, Josef
Two essays   GEN   3 trb

BLANK, Allan
Four pieces   OKM   2 trp, 3 trb

CUSTER, Arthur
Concerto for brass
quintet GEN
3 pieces for 6 brass
instruments GEN

DIEMENTE, Edward
Designs   SEM   trp, trb
1. Small swirls,
gentle swirls
2. Dots and dashes
3. Landscape
4. Images flying about
5. Blurs and smudges

DONAHUE, Robert
    Little suite   WIM   trp, hn, trb
    Prelude. Dirge.
    Toccata.

FLAGELLO, Nicolas
    Philos for brass
    quintet   GEN

GARLICK, Antony
    Suite for brass en-   2 trp, hn,
    semble SEM   trb

HEUSSENSTAMM, George
    Museum piece SEM   8 hn, 6 trp,
    (see also "Percus-   6 trb, 2 tba,
    sion")   4 perc
    Tubafour SEM   4 tba

KUPFERMAN, Meyer
    Brass quintet GEN
    Concertino for 11   2 hn, 4 trp,
    brass instruments 4 trb, tba
    GEN

LEICHTLING, Alan
    Bagatelles for brass
    quintet, Op. 52 SEM

LEVY, Frank
    Brass quintet SEM

McKAY, George Frederick
    Allegro scherzozo   4 trb
    CLB

RAPHLING, Sam
    Three pieces for   instr not
    brass trio GEN   available

REIF, Paul
    Brass quintet SEM

RUSSELL, Robert
    Abstract No. 2 GEN   2 trp (or
                           2 hn)

STEINER, Gitta
    Brass quintet SEM

SYDEMAN, William
    Brass quintet OKM
    Fanfare and variations 2 trp, 2
    OKM   trb
    Music for low brass 3 trb, tba
    OKM
    Tower music for brass
    quintet OKM
    Trio for treble instru-
    ments OKM

WHITTENBERG, Charles
    Triptych for brass
    quintet GEN

4. BIG BAND CONCERT JAZZ

WARD, Russell
    Preservation rock TP   conductor (pno, gtr, org, acdn), 2 a-
                                  sax, 2 t-sax, bar-sax, 4 trp, 4 trb,
                                  b-gtr, tba, dr

    Sand, man TP   instr same as above for "Preserva-
                                    tion rock"

5. PERCUSSION

BECK, John Ness and Don Jones
    Rhapsody for percussion and band   (may be played by 1 or 2 percussion
    KMI (see also "Band")   soloists)

CARNO, Zita
    Sextet for percussion for   instr not available
    6 players MP

DE BERADINIS, John
    Dialogues for violin and per-
    cussion SEM

DELP, Ron
  Dreams, 1970   SEM   fl, cl, c-b, 4 perc

DIEMENTE, Edward
  For miles and miles   SEM   solo vib
  Quartet   SEM   sax, trb, c-b, perc
  Trio   SEM   fl, trp, perc
  Unvelopment   SEM   c-b (solo), 3 sax, electric gtr,
                                     cel, 2 perc

DUCKWORTH, William
  Gambit   CPC   instr not available

FARBERMAN, Harold
  Alea: a game of chance for   instr not available
    6 players   GEN

FRAZEUR, Theodore
  UHURU: a percussion ballet   includes instr of pitched metalic
    KMI   sounds (bells, brake dr, tuned pipes,
                                     cowbells, chimes); 5 timp

HEUSSENSTAMM, George
  Double solo for clarinet and
    percussion   SEM
  Museum piece   SEM   8 hn, 6 trp, 6 trb, 2 tba, 4 perc
  Music for three   SEM   amplified b-fl, vib, perc
  Poikilos   SEM   fl, vib, perc

HODKINSON, Sydney
  Drawings: set No. 3   MP   cl, dr

MASONER, E. L.
  Trio for percussion   KMI   tam, bongos, bells

MILLER, Malloy
  Two rituals (for 5 players) MP   instr not available

RAPHLING, Sam
  Suite for solo percussion and   Part I: tam, wood blocks, cmb,
    piano   BI   castanets
                                     Part II: tri, b-dr, temple blocks,
                                              sn-dr
RUSSELL, Armand
  2nd concerto for percussion RMP   6 players utilizing different metal,
                                     wood and mixed sounds

SCHINSTINE, William J.
  Synco-stix for snare drum solo   sn-dr
    SMC

STEINER, Gitta
  Four bagatelles for solo vibra-   vib
    phone   SEM
  Quartet for percussion   SEM   instr not available
  Trio for piano and 2 percus-   pno, perc
    sionists   SEM

SYDEMAN, William
  Duo for trumpet and percussion   trp, perc
    OKM
  Quintet OKM   hn(or trb), cl, pno, c-b, perc
  Trio OKM   fl, c-b, perc

REIF, Paul
  Eulogy for a friend SEM   str orch & perc

6. ORCHESTRA

STRING AND CHAMBER ORCHESTRA (WITH AND WITHOUT SOLO)

FRACKENPOHL, Arthur
  Suite GS(R)   trp; str   timing NA

REIF, Paul
  Eulogy for a friend for string   15 min
    orchestra and percussion SEM

STEINER, Gitta
  Tetrark for string orchestra   6 min
    SEM(R)

SYDEMAN, William
  Concert piece OKM(R)   hn; str   10 min
  Concertino OKM(R)   ob, pno; str 10 min
  Concerto da camera OKM(R) vla; cham   10 min
  Concerto da camera No. 2   vln; cham   14 min
    OKM(R)
  Largo OKM(R)   vlc; str   6 min

FULL SYMPHONY ORCHESTRA (WITH AND WITHOUT SOLO)

ASCHAFFENBURG, Walter
  Three dances for orchestra TP(R)   NA

LEWIS, Robert Hall
  Designs for orchestra TP(R)   NA

PERSICHETTI, Vincent
  Night dances EV(R)   NA
  Sinfonia: Janiculum EV(R)   NA

ROREM, Ned
  Piano concerto in 6 movements   pno   NA
    B&H(R)
    Strands. Five. Whispers.
    Sighs. Lava. Sparks.

STARER, Robert
  Six variations with twelve   5
    notes MCA(R)

STEINER, Gitta
  Concerto SEM(R)   pno   15 min

7. BAND
(Including Wind Symphony)

BECK, John Ness and Don Jones
Rhapsody for percussion and
  band   KMI
(see also "Percussion")
one or two solo   9 min
percussionists

BENSON, Warren
Solitary dancer   MCA   6.5 min

CACAVAS, John
Theme and rockout   4.5 min
  CHAP

COLE, George
Maelstrom (a pavane   5.5 min
  for our age)   EBM

DILLON, Robert
Quartz mountain: 3.5 min
  overture   CLB

ERICKSON, Frank
Walden: pastorale for   4.5 min
  band   CHAP

FRACKENPOHL, Arthur
Quintagon (5 pieces for   8 min
  band)   EV
1. Fanfare (brass and
   percussion)
2. Lullaby (woodwinds)
3. Canon
4. Dirge
5. Rondo

GOLD, Ernest
Fugue, gavotte and march   6 min
  EBM

GRUNDMAN, Clare
American folk rhapsody   7 min
  No. 3   B&H

HARTLEY, Walter S.
Capriccio for trombone   NA
  and band   JBI

JARRETT, Jack
Holiday for horns   CLB   4 min
  hn qrt and band

KURKA, Robert
Good soldier Schweik suite   7 min
  WEIN

LOCKWOOD, Normand
A ballad of the North   25 min
  and South   AMP
Carol fantasy   AMP   15 min

McBETH, W. Francis
Divergents   SMC   NA
Drammatico   SMC   5 min

MITCHELL, Rex
Introduction and fantasia   6.5 min
  EBM

NIXON, Roger
Prelude and fugue   CF   5 min

REED, Alfred
A jubilant overture   CLB   6 min

SPEARS, Jared
Chatham overture   SMC   4 min

SYDEMAN, William
Double concerto for   13 min
  trumpet, trombone
  band and strings OKM(R)

WARRINGTON, John
Waltzing sombrero   TP   1.5 min

WHEAR, Paul W.
Kensington: overture   3.5 min
  CLB

KEY TO ADDITIONAL PUBLISHERS FOR ADDENDUM

LM   Lyra Music
      133 West 69th Street
      New York, N. Y.   10023

OKM   Okra Music Corporation
      177 East 87th Street
      New York, N. Y.   10028

PJS   Paul J. Sifler
      3947 Fredonia Drive
      Hollywood 28, California

RMP   Rochester Music Photocopy Co.
      12 Worthington Road
      Rochester, N. Y.   14622

Amendments to the Second Edition

In order to correct the second edition and bring it up to date, some amendments are listed below. Not only have errors of omission and commission been corrected, but many publisher designations have also been changed. This latter reflects the exchange of various publishing rights among the publishers as well as errors in the second edition.

Page

10   BACON (cont): publisher of "Is there such a thing as day?" is AMP

14   CAGE: publisher of "The wonderful widow of eighteen springs" is CFP

16   CORY: change first name to "George"

29   IVES: after "From Lincoln the great commoner" change NME to PIC

41   READ: after "From a lute of jade" change HE to SMC

42   ROREM: after "Four dialogues" change CFP to B&H

47   THOMSON: after "La belle en dormant" change GS to B&H

52   BACON: after "The long farewell" change SHAW to EBM

63   CHAFLIN: change spelling to "CLAFLIN"

64   COPLAND: change solo for "Lark" from "B" to "Bar"

88   LATHAM: accompaniment for "A prophecy of peace" should read "fl, ob, cl, 2 hn, 3 trp, bsn, perc; or org"

89   LEVY: after "Our Father" change COL to B&H

98   NIXON: after "The wind" change TP to L-G

99   PERSICHETTI: change author of text of "The pleiades" to Walt Whitman

103   READ: enter the song "Complaint" under Reed, Alfred

107   SCHUMAN: accompaniment for "Choruses from The Mighty Casey" is "pno-4 hands"

124   DELLO JOIO: change entry no. 3 to read "Holy Infant's lullaby"

129   IVES: after "Lincoln the great commoner" change TP to PIC

135   PINKHAM: change chorus of "A litany" from "SS" to "SA"

POWELL: after "Sweet lovers love the spring" change CF to COL

136 READ: after "The moon" change AMP to CF

141 CHENOWETH: change spelling of first name to "Wilbur"

146 IVES: after "Lincoln the great commoner" change TP to PIC

158 FINNEY: change duration of "Pilgrim psalms" from "30" to "14"

162 LATHAM: accompaniment for "A prophecy of peace" should read "fl, ob, cl, bsn, 2 hn, 3 trp, perc"

164 MENNIN: after both entries add "(R)" after CF

177 FAREWELL: change spelling to "FARWELL"
FOSS: after "Four two-voiced inventions" change GS to CF

178 FULEIHAN (cont): after "Harvest chant" change GS to SMPC

182 MacDOWELL: after "Four little poems" change AMP to GS; after "Sonata No. 1 'Tragica'" change KAL to GS; after "Sonata No. 2, 'Eroica'" change AMP to GS; after "Woodland sketches" change AMP to GS

186 SUBOTNIK: after "Prelude No. 4" change AMP to MCA
THOMSON: after "Etudes" change CF to GS; after "Portraits" change MER to GS

187 CAGE: after first and third entry delete word "prepared"

191 CLAFFLIN: change spelling to "CLAFLIN"

197 COPLAND: after "Nocturne (1926)" change AMP to B&H

203 FULEIHAN: after "Recitative and scilienne" change GS to SMPC

205 BAILEY: after "Sonata Op. 3" change CF to TP

206 HELM: after "Sonata" change B&H to AMP

215 JACOBI: after "Meditation" change W-7 to SMPC

217 MOEVS: change instrumentation of "Variazioni sopra una melodia" to read "vla, vlc"

222 THOMPSON: after "Quartet No. 1" change ECS to CF

223 LEOFFLER: change spelling to "LOEFFLER"

224 RANCY: change spelling to "RANEY"

226 DIAMOND: after "Quintet" change CF to SMPC

228 KUBIK: after "Divertimento No. 2" change COL to MCA

234 PISTON: after "Three pieces" change NME to AMP
SCHULLER: after "Duo sonata" change BB to AMP

241 GRUENBERG: after "Creation" add "solo voice" and "text by
James Weldon Johnson"

244 PRESSER: after "Suite" change "3 trp" to "3 tba"

260 KRAFT: after "Momentum for 8 percussionists" change SMPC to SMC

277 FOOTE: after "A night piece" change S-B to SMC

283 BERNSTEIN: change duration of "Symphonic dances from West Side
Story" from "10" to "22"

284 COWELL: after "Overture" change SMPC(R) to PIC(R)

285 DUKELSKY: after "Symphony No. 3" change COL(R) to CF(R)

286 FULEIHAN: after "Mediterranean suite" change GS to SMPC
GORDAN: change spelling to "GORDON"

289: KAY: change spelling of first name to "Hershy"

293: STILL: after "Afro-American Symphony" change JF(R) to HWG(R)

294: THOMPSON: after both entries change ECS to CF(R)

297: DELLO JOIO: change duration of "Lamentation of Saul" from "5"
to "18"

298 FOSS: after "Song of songs" change GS to CF(R)

307 JOHNSON: change spelling of first name to "Lockrem"

337 BEREZOWSKY: change page citation from 224 to 225

338 BLACKWOOD: change page citation from 224 to 225
BROWN: change page citation from 224 to 225

340 FRANCO: change page citation from 125 to 126

341 HANNAS: change spelling to "HANNAHS"

342 JOHNSON: change spelling of first name to "Lockrem"
KAY: change spelling of first name to "Hershy"

344 MALTLEY: change spelling to "MALTBY"

345 RANCY: change spelling to "RANEY"

KEY TO PUBLISHERS

AB   Alexander Broude, Inc.
      1619 Broadway
      New York, N. Y. 10019

ABP   Abington Press
      201 8th Avenue South
      Nashville, Tennessee 37202

AMC   Alfred Music Co., Inc.
      75 Channel Drive
      Port Washington, N. Y. 11050

AMP   Associated Music Publishers,
      609 Fifth Avenue   Inc.
      New York, N. Y. 10017
        Agents overseas:
        Albania, Austria, Bulgaria,
        Czechoslovakia, Greece,
        Hungary, Poland, Rumania,
        Yugoslavia:...Doblinger,
        Vienna, Austria
        Australia:...Allan & Co. Ltd.,
        Melbourne
        Belgium, Netherlands,
        Switzerland, West Germany:
        ...B. Schott's Soehne,
        Mainz, Germany
        Denmark, Finland, Norway,
        Sweden:...Wilhelm Hansen,
        Copenhagen, Denmark
        France:...Editions Max
        Eschig, Paris
        Italy:...G. Ricordi, Milan
        Spain:...Union Musical
        Española, Madrid
        United Kingdom & Irish
        Free State:...Schott & Co.
        Ltd., London

Arno Arno Press
      330 Madison Ave.
      New York, N. Y.
      10017

AUG   Augsburg Publishing House
      426 South Fifth Street
      Minneapolis, Minnesota
      55415

BB   Broude Brothers Limited
      Music Publishers
      56 West 45th Street
      New York, N. Y. 10036

BCM   Bowdoin College Music Press
      New Brunswick, Maine

BEL   Belwin, Inc.
      Rockville Center, N. Y. 11571

B&H   Boosey & Hawkes
      30 West 57th Street
      New York, N. Y. 10019
      (for rental); for sales, address:
      Oceanside, New York, N. Y.
      11572
        Agents overseas:
        Australia:...Boosey & Hawkes
        (Australia) Pty. Ltd., Sydney
        Austria:...Theater-Verlag
        Eirich, Vienna
        Belgium & France:...Boosey
        & Hawkes, S.A., Paris
        Canada:...Boosey & Hawkes
        (Canada) Ltd., Toronto
        Denmark:...Wilhelm Hansen,
        Copenhagen
        England:...Boosey & Hawkes
        Music Publishers Ltd.,
        London
        Germany & Switzerland:...
        Boosey & Hawkes GmbH,
        Bonn
        Hungary:...Kultura, Budapest
        Italy:...Carisch S. p. a.,
        Milan
        Netherlands:...Albersen &
        Co., The Hague
        Norway:...Norsk Musikforlag
        a/s, Oslo
        South Africa:...Boosey &
        Hawkes (S. Africa) Pty.
        Ltd., Johannesburg
        South America:...Barry &
        Cia, Buenos Aires,
        Argentina
        Spain:...Robert Achard,
        Madrid
        Sweden:...Carl Gehrmans
        Musikforlag, Stockholm

BI	Bourne Co. (formerly Bourne, 136 West 52nd Street Inc.) New York, N. Y. 10019	COL	Franco Colombo Publications A Division of Belwin, Inc. 16 West 61st Street New York, N. Y. 10023 Agents overseas: Australia:...G. Ricordi & Co., Sydney Argentina:...Ricordi Americana S.A., Buenos Aires Brazil:...Ricordi Brasileira S.A., São Paulo Canada:...Leeds Music Ltd., Toronto England:...G. Ricordi & Co. (London) Ltd. London France:...Edition Salabert, Paris Germany:...G. Ricordi & Co., Frankfurt/Main Italy:...G. Ricordi & Co., Milan Mexico:...G. Ricordi & Co., Mexico City, D. F. Switzerland:...Symphonia Verlag, Basel
BOS	The Boston Music Company 116 Boylston Street Boston, Mass. 02116		
CBP	Claude Benny Press Box 461 Milton Junction, Wisconsin 53563		
CF	Carl Fischer, Inc. 56-62 Cooper Square New York, N. Y. 10003		
CFP	C. F. Peters Corporation 373 Park Avenue South New York, N. Y. 10016 Agents overseas: Austria & Germany:...C. F. Peters, Frankfurt/Main Belgium:...Schott Frères, Brussels Norway:...Harold Lyche & Co., Oslo Switzerland:...Edition Eulenburg, Zurich All other countries:... Hinrichsen Edition Ltd., London with following exception: Countries of Western Hemisphere, Japan and The Philippines, which should order C. F. Peters publications from the office in New York, N. Y.		
		CPC	M. M. Cole Publishing Co. 251 East Grand Avenue Chicago, Illinois 60611
		CPE	Composer/Performer Edition 330 University Avenue Davis, California 05616
		CPH	Concordia Publishing House 358 South Jefferson Avenue St. Louis, Missouri 63118
		CPI	The Composers Press, Inc. c/o Robert B. Brown Music Co. 1709 No. Kenmore Avenue Hollywood, California 90027
CHAP	Chappell & Co., Inc. 609 Fifth Avenue New York, N. Y. 10017 Agents overseas: Australia:...Chappell & Co. Ltd., Sydney England:...Chappell & Co. Ltd., London France:...S.A.F. Chappell, Paris		
		DCP	Da Capo Press 227 West 17th Street New York, N. Y. 10011
		EBM	Edward B. Marks Music Corp. 136 West 52nd Street New York, N. Y. 10019 Agent overseas: England:...Schott & Co. Ltd., London
CLB	C. L. Barnhouse Co. Music Publishers Oskaloosa, Iowa 52577		
		ECS	E. C. Schirmer Music Company 600 Washington Street Boston, Mass. 02111

135

EM	Edition Musicus 333 West 52nd Street New York, N. Y. 10019	GS	G. Schirmer, Inc. 609 Fifth Avenue New York, N. Y. 10017 Agents overseas:
EV	Elkan-Vogel Co. A subsidiary of Theodore Presser Co. Presser Place Bryn Mawr, Pa. 19010 Sole agents in U.S.A. Durand Edition Henry Lemoine & Co., Jean Jobert Editions Philippo. Ars Nova Organ catalogue: Edition Heuwekemeijer.		Australia:...Allan & Co. Ltd., Melbourne (for orch & opera rental materials) Austria:...Universal Edition, Vienna (for orch & opera rental materials) Denmark, Norway, Sweden: ...Wilhelm Hansen, Copenhagen England:...Chappell & Co. Ltd., London (materials for sale); J. Curwen & Sons, Ltd; Faber Music Ltd.
FAM	Fine Arts Music Press Tulsa, Oklahoma		France also for Belgium, Czechoslovakia, Greece, Hungary, Israel, Poland, Portugal, Spain & Yugo-
FER	Ferol Publications Box 6007 Alexandria, Va. 22306		slavia:...Edition Salabert, Paris (for orch & opera rentals)
FLAM	Harold Flammer, Inc. c/o Shawnee Press Delaware Gap, Pa. 18327		Germany:...Anton Benjamin, Hamburg (for orch rentals); August Seith, Munich (ma- terials for sale)
FM	Frank Music Corp. c/o The Boston Music Co. 116 Boylston Street Boston, Mass. 02116 Agents overseas: Brazil:...Fermata Do Brazil LTDA, São Paulo		Italy:...G. Ricordi & Co., Milan Netherlands:...Albersen & Co., The Hague (for orch rentals)
	Canada:...Frank Music Co. (Canada) Ltd., Toronto England:...Frank Music	HAR	Hargail Music Press 157 West 57th Street New York, N. Y. 10019
	Company Ltd., London Italy:...Edizioni Frank Music S.r.l., Milan Re: Mexico:...Ariston Music Inc., New York, N. Y.	HE	Henri Elkan Music Publisher 1316 Walnut Street Philadelphia, Pa. 19107 Agent overseas: Belgium:...metropolis Frankrijklei 24, Antwerpen 1
GAL	Galaxy Music Corporation 2121 Broadway New York, N. Y. 10023 Agents overseas: England:...Galliard Ltd., London	HME	Helios Music Edition c/o Mark Foster Music Co. Box 783 Marquette, Michigan 49855
	Germany:...Heinrichshofen's verlag, Wilhelmshaven	HWG	The H. W. Gray Company, Inc. 159 East 48th Street New York, N. Y. 10017
GEN	General Music Publishing Co., The Boston Music Co. Inc. (sole distributor) 116 Boylston Street Boston, Mass. 02116		Agent overseas: England:...Novello & Co., Ltd., London

IP	Independent Publishers 215 East 42nd Street New York, N. Y. 10019		England:... Mills Music Ltd., London France:... Mills France, Paris
JBI	Joseph Boonin, Inc. 831 Main Street Hackensack, New Jersey 07601		Germany:... Mills Musikver- lag GmbH, Berlin-Halensee Netherlands:... Mills-Holland N.V., Amsterdam
JF	J. Fischer & Bro. Harristown Road Glen Rock, New Jersey 07452		Spain & Portugal:... Editorial Mills Music Española, Madrid
KAL	Edwin F. Kalmus 1345 New York Avenue Huntington Station, L. I., N. Y. 11748	MJQ	MJQ Music, Inc. 200 West 57th Street New York, N. Y. 10019
KING	Robert King Music Company North Easton, Mass. 02356	MM	McGinnis & Marx 201 West 86th Street, Apt. 706 New York, N. Y. 10024
KMI	Kendor Music, Inc. Delevan, N. Y. 14042	MP	Music for Percussion, Inc. 17 West 60th Street New York, N. Y. 10023
KSM	KSM Publishing Co. 507 North Willomet Dallas, Texas 75208	MPC	Mark Press Company c/o Mark Foster Music Co. Box 783 Marquette, Michigan 49855
L-G	Lawson-Gould Music Publishers Inc., G. Schirmer, sole selling agent. 609 Fifth Avenue New York, N. Y. 10017	NAK	Neil A. Kjos Music Publishers 525 Busse Highway Park Ridge, Illinois 60068
LPI	Leblanc Publications, Inc. Kenosha, Wisconsin	OPB	O. Pagani and Bros., Inc. 289 Bleecker Street New York, N. Y. 10014
LMP	Ludwig Music Publishing Co. 557-67 East 140th Street Cleveland, Ohio 44110	OX	Oxford University Press 200 Madison Avenue New York, N. Y. 10016
MCA	Music Corporation of America 543 West 43rd Street New York, N. Y. 10036	PIC	Peer International Corporation c/o Southern Music Publishing 1619 Broadway Co. New York, N. Y. 10019
MER	Mercury Music Corporation c/o Theodore Presser Company Presser Place Bryn Mawr, Pa. 19010	RBB	Robert B. Brown Music Co. 1709 No. Kenmore Avenue Hollywood, California 90027
MIL	Mills Music, Inc. 1790 Broadway New York, N. Y. 10019 Agents overseas: Central & South America:... Editora Musical Mills Ltda, São Paulo, Brazil; Mills Music de Mexico, Mexico City, D. F.	RDR S-B	R. D. Row Music Company 353 Newbury Street Boston 15, Mass. Summy-Birchard Company 1834 Ridge Avenue Evanston, Illinois 60204

S-C Scully-Cutter Urtext Editions
1315 4th Street Southeast
Minneapolis, Minnesota 55414

SEM Seesaw Music Corporation
177 East 87th Street
New York, N. Y. 10028

SF Sam Fox Publishing Co., Inc.
1841 Broadway
New York, N. Y. 10023

SHAW Shawnee Press, Inc.
Delaware Water Gap, Pa.
18327

SMC Southern Music Company
1100 Broadway--P.O. Box 329
San Antonio, Texas 78206

SMP The Sacred Music Press
501 East 3rd Street
Dayton, Ohio 45401

SMPC Southern Music Publishing, Co.,
1619 Broadway
New York, N. Y. 10019
Agents overseas:
Australia:...Southern Music
Publishing Company (Aus-
tralasia) Pty. Ltd., Sydney
Canada:...Southern Music
Publishing Company (Canada)
Ltd., Montreal
Central & South America:...
Ricordi Americana, S. A.
Buenos Aires, Argentina
European countries:...Peer
Musikverlag GmbH, Ham-
burg, Germany
Japan:...Nippon Gakki Co.
Ltd. Gakufu, Ginza 7-1,
Chuo-Ku, Tokyo
Mexico:...Promotoro His-
pana Americana de Musica,
Mexico City, D. F.
New Zealand:...Southern
Music Publishing Company
(New Zealand) Pty. Ltd.,
Auckland C. 1

TP Theodore Presser Company
Presser Place
Bryn Mawr, Pa. 19010
Agents overseas:
Austria:...Universal Edition,
Vienna; Haydn Mozart
Press, Vienna; Philhar-

monia Pocket Scores, Vienna
England:...Universal Edition,
London
France:...Editions Musicales
Transatlantiques, Paris;
Heugel & Cie, Paris-
Germany:...Impero Verlag,
Wilhelmshaven
Switzerland:...Universal
Edition, Zurich

UCP University of California Press
Berkeley, California 94720

UMP University of Miami Press
Miami, Florida

VAL The New Valley Music Press
Sage Hall, Smith College
Northampton, Mass. 01060

VB Volkwein Bros., Inc.
117 Sandusky Street
Pittsburgh, Pa. 15212

WEIN Weintraub Music Company
33 West 60th Street
New York, N. Y. 10023

WIM Western International Music, Inc.
2859 Holt Avenue
Los Angeles, California 90034

WIT M. Witmark and Sons
488 Madison Avenue
New York, N. Y. 10022

WLP World Library Publications, Inc.
2145 Central Parkway
Cincinnati, Ohio 45214

WMC Walton Music Corp.
17 West 60th Street
New York, N. Y. 10023

WME Waldwick Music Editions
123 Bergen Avenue
Waldick, New Jersey 07463

W-7 Warner Bros.--Seven Arts Music
488 Madison Avenue
New York, N. Y. 10022

YUP Yale University Press
92A Yale Station
New Haven, Connecticut
06520

AUTHOR INDEX

COMPOSER INDEX

A

Abramson, Robert 61
Adler, Samuel (1928-) 9, 17, 44, 53, 67, 80, 85, 103, 107
Aitken, Hugh 61, 67, 68, 70, 71, 97, 107
Albright, William 64
Allanbrook, Douglas (1921-) 61, 101
Alexander, Joseph (1910-) 68, 73, 84, 126
Anderson, Garland 71
Antheil, George (1900-1959) 61
Applebaum, Edward 75
Argento, Dominick 9, 17, 63, 99, 105
Arnatt, Ronald 64
Arnold, Hubert 81
Aschaffenburg, Walter 129
Auerback, Norman 44
Avshalomov, Jacob (1919-) 17, 101

B

Babin, Stanley 61
Bach, Jan 88
Bacon, Ernst (1898-) 44
Baksa, Robert F. 9, 44, 68, 77
Balbo, G. C. 77
Bales, Richard (1915-) 88, 97, 98
Ballard, Louis W. 17
Barab, Seymour (1921-) 44, 77, 99, 105
Barati, George (1913-) 75
Barber, Samuel (1910-) 17, 45, 85, 101, 107
Barker, John Nelson 105
Baron, Samuel 84
Bartow, Nevett 17, 64
Bassett, Leslie (1923-) 71, 73, 81, 82, 101
Bauernschmidt, Robert 88
Baumgartner, H. Leroy 17, 18
Bavicchi, John (1922-) 45, 69, 70
Beach, Bennie 84
Beck, John Ness (1930-) 9, 115, 127, 130
Beeson, Jack (1921-) 9, 18, 45, 50, 61, 67, 101, 116
Beglarian, Grant (1927-) 18, 107
Belcher, Supply (1751-1836) 18

Bellson, Louis 88
Benaglia, John 78
Bencriscutto, Frank 88
Bennett, David 18, 71, 78, 103, 107, 122
Bennett, Robert Russell 107
Benson, Warren 18, 88, 107, 121, 130
Bergsma, William (1921-) 98, 101
Berkowitz, Leonard 18, 45, 53, 107
Berkowitz, Sol 18, 107
Berlinski, Herman (1910-) 18, 64, 77, 82
Bernstein, Seymour 61
Berry, Wallace (1928-) 19
Beveridge, Thomas 116, 120
Beyer, Frederick 82
Bialowsky, Marshall (1923-) 77
Bielawa, Herbert 45, 107
Billings, William (1746-1800) 19, 45
Bingham, Seth (1882-) 64
Binkerd, Gordon (1916-) 9, 19, 45, 46, 50, 61, 64, 68, 74, 75, 77, 81, 85, 101
Blakley, D. Duane 19, 53
Blank, Allan (1925-) 50, 116, 122, 124, 126
Bliss, J. A. 10
Blitzstein, Marc (1905-1964) 20, 53
Blumenfeld, Harold 80
Boatwright, Howard 116
Boda, John (1922-) 68, 82
Boeringer, James (1930-) 20, 78
Bolcom, William 61
Bowles, Paul 10
Boyd, Jack 20
Brant, Henry (1913-) 81, 88
Briccetti, Thomas (1936-) 72
Bright, Houston (1916-) 20, 21, 46, 50, 53
Brindel, Bernard 71
Bristow, George (1825-1898) 105
Britain, Radie (1903-) 80, 82
Brown, Earle (1926-) 63, 74, 88
Brown, Newel Kay (1932-) 77
Brown, Rayner (1912-) 21, 64, 68, 73, 80, 82, 84, 107, 124
Brown, Thomas 88, 107
Browne, Donald 88
Brubeck, Dave (1920-) 21, 61, 116, 120

143

144

147

149

Vaughan, Clifford 68
Vaughan, Rodger 82
Vazzana, Anthony 71
Velke, Fritz (1930-) 112
Vercoe, Barry 41, 59
Vernon, Knight 49
Verrall, John (1908-) 66, 81
Vierra, M. L. 42
Vincent, John (1902-) 100
Vore, Val S. 96

W

Wagner, Joseph (1900-) 66, 74,
75, 85, 112
Walker, Richard (1912-) 78, 79,
112
Walton, Kenneth 49
Ward, Robert (1917-) 103, 104,
112
Ward, Russell 127
Ward-Steinman, David (1936-) 63,
80
Warren, Elinor Remick (1905-)
42, 49
Warrington, John 91, 109, 130
Washburn, Robert (1928-) 42, 75,
80, 82, 97, 112
Watson, Walter (1933-) 50
Weast, Robert 72
Weathers, Keith (1943-) 66
Weaver, John 42, 66
Weber, Ben (1916-) 68, 77
Weille, F. Blair 85
Weiner, Lawrence 42, 59, 97, 113
Weiner, Stanley (1925-) 100
Weisgall, Hugo (1912-) 63, 106
Weiss, Edward 113
Werle, Floyd E. 113
Wernick, Richard 77
Westergaard, Peter 106
Whear, Paul W. (1925-) 42, 59,
73, 83, 113, 130
White, Donald H. 42, 73, 81, 113
White, John 16
White, Louie L. 66
Whithorne, Emerson (1884-1958) 75,
103
Whittenberg, Charles 68, 71, 72,
127
Wienhorst, Richard (1920-) 42
Wilder, Alec (1907-) 72
Williams, Clifton 96, 113
Williams, David Howard 42, 43
Williams, Jan 96
Williams, Kent J. 96
Willis, Richard 75, 113
Wolfe, Christian (1934-) 77, 125
Wolford, Darwin 66

Woolf, Gregory 119, 121
Woollen, Russell (1923-) 66
Work, John W. 43, 60
Wuensh, Gerhard (1925-) 66
Wuorinen, Charles 63, 64
Wyton, Alex 43, 66

Y

Yardumian, Richard (1917-) 43,
60
York, Walter Wynn 43
Yoshioka, Emmett 73
Young, Gordon 66
Young, Michael E. 66

Z

Zabrak, Harold 63
Zaninelli, Luigi (1932-) 43, 60,
80, 86
Zimmerman, Phyllis 43